Cristine Rose and Lisa Banes in a scene from the Playwrights Horizons production of "Isn't it Romantic."

PHOTO BY PETER CUNNINGHAM

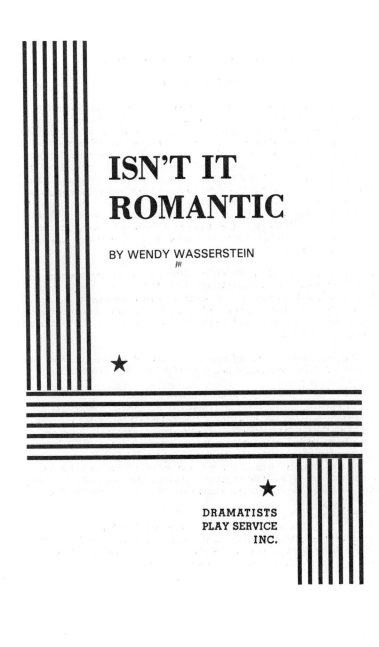

ISN'T IT ROMANTIC

BY WENDY WASSERSTEIN

★

★

DRAMATISTS
PLAY SERVICE
INC.

ISN'T IT ROMANTIC was presented by Playwright's Horizons, in New York City, December 15, 1983. It was directed by Gerald Gutierrez; the scenery was designed by Andrew Jackness; costumes were designed by Ann Emonts; lighting was designed by James F. Ingalls; production stage manager was J. Thomas Vivian; sound was designed by Scott Lehrer; music coordination by Jack Feldman; choreography by Susan Rosenstock.

JANIE BLUMBERG.....................................Cristine Rose
HARRIET CORNWALL...............................Lisa Banes
MARTY STERLING.....................................Chip Zien
TASHA BLUMBERG...............................Betty Comden
SIMON BLUMBERG.........................Stephen Pearlman
LILLIAN CORNWALL............................Jo Henderson
PAUL STUART.......................................Jerry Lanning
VLADIMIR...Tom Robbins

TELEPHONE MESSAGES

SCHLOMO...Timmy Geissler
HART FARRELL...................................Kevin Kline
JULIE STERN.....................................Swoosie Kurtz
TAJLEI KAPLAN SINGLEBERRY.......................Patti Lupone
OPERATOR...Ellis Rabb
CYNTHIA PETERSON.....................................Meryl Streep
MILTY STERLING..Jerry Zaks

ISN'T IT ROMANTIC was commissioned in 1979 by The Phoenix Theatre in New York. It was presented, in an earlier version, by the Phoenix Theatre, in New York City, May 28, 1981. It was directed by Steven Robman; the scenery was designed by Marjorie Bradley Kellogg; costumes were designed by Jennifer Von Mayrhauser and Denise Romano; lighting was designed by Spencer Mosse.

JANIE BLUMBERG...Alma Cuervo
HARRIET CORNWALL................................Laurie Kennedy
SALVATORE..Fritz Kupfer
TASHA BLUMBERG...Jane Hoffman
SIMON BLUMBERG....................................Bernie Passeltiner
LILLIAN CORNWALL.....................................Barbara Baxley
MARTY STERLING..Peter Riegert
PAUL STUART...Bob Gunton
VLADIMIR...Fritz Kupfer

For André and Gerry who made it possible
for me to dedicate this play

To My Parents

Characters

(in order of appearance)

Janie Blumberg
Harriet Cornwall
Marty Sterling
Tasha Blumberg
Simon Blumberg
Lillian Cornwall
Paul Stuart
Vladimir

The play takes place in 1983 in New York, New York. The action is set in various locations in Manhattan and the set should reflect the variety of locales.

In Mr. Gutierrez's production at Playwrights Horizons four men dressed as moving men, waiters, joggers etc., shifted the sets for each scene. Thus the scene changes were incorporated into the production and often concluded during the phone message segments.

4

ISN'T IT ROMANTIC

PROLOGUE

Music and sounds of Manhattan fade into a voice on a phone machine. Phone machine segments occur between scenes. There is no action during these prologue messages.

JANIE. Hi, this is Janie Blumberg. I'm not in right now, but if you leave me your name and number I should be able to get back to you sometime today or tomorrow. (*She sings.*) Isn't it romantic, merely to be young on such a night as this, isn't it romantic every something something is like a . . . (*The machine cuts off.*)

TASHA & SIMON. (*Ring, Beep. They sing.*) "Is this the little girl I carried. Is this the little boy at play. I don't remember growing older, when did they."* (*Tasha's voice.*) This is your darling mother, I wanted to welcome you to your new apartment. Call me sweetheart, your father wants to talk to you. (*Hang up.*)

HARRIET. (*Beep.*) Hi Janie, it's Harriet. I can't help you unpack tonight. I have a job interview early tomorrow morning. Can you have breakfast with me afterwards? I'll meet you across the street from Rumpelmeyers at ten. Oh, I ran into Cynthia Peterson on the street, I gave her your number. Please don't hate me. Bye. (*Hang up.*)

SIMON. (*Beep.*) Uh, Janie, it's your father. Uh, er, uh, call your mother. (*Hang up.*)

CYNTHIA PETERSON. (*Beep.*) Janie, it's Cynthia Peterson. Harriet told me you moved to New York. Why haven't you called me? Everything is awful. I'm getting divorced, I'm looking for a job, there are no men. Call me. Let's have lunch. (*Hang up.*)

TASHA & SIMON. (*They sing.*) "Sunrise, sunset. Sunrise, sunset. Quickly flow the day. . . ." (*Dial tone.*)

MAN'S VOICE. (*Operator.*) Please hang up. There seems to be a receiver off the hook.

*See Special Note on copyright page.

ACT ONE

Scene One

Central Park South. Janie Blumberg, 28, is sitting on a park bench. Her appearance is a little kooky, a little sweet, a little unconfident, all of which some might call creative. Or even witty. There is a trash can D.R. We hear "Hi ho, hi ho, it's off to work we go . . ." Harriet enters from L., singing. Harriet could be the cover girl on the best working women's magazine. She is attractive, very bright, charming and easily put together. Harriet spots Janie.

HARRIET. Hi ho, hi ho, it's off to work we go. . . . I think I got the job. (*They hug.*) Hi Janie.

JANIE. Hi, Harriet.

HARRIET. Thank God you're here.

JANIE. Of course I'm here. I got your message last night.

HARRIET. The man I interviewed with was very impressed I took a year off in Italy to look at pictures. I liked him. He was cold, aloof, distant. Very sexy. Can I have a hit of your Tab?

JANIE. Sure.

HARRIET. I can't stay for breakfast. I told him I could come right back to Colgate for a second interview. Janie, I think our move back home to New York is going to be very successful.

JANIE. It is.

HARRIET. Of course there's absolutely no reason why you should believe me.

JANIE. You have an M.B.A. from Harvard. Of course I believe you.

HARRIET. You sound like your mother.

JANIE. No. Tasha would believe you cause you're thin. Look at us. You look like a Vermeer and I look like a extra in Potemkin.

HARRIET. Janie, I think someone's watching us.

JANIE. (*Fluffing her hair.*) Do I look all right? You know what I resent?

6

HARRIET. What?

JANIE. Just about everything except you. I resent having to pay the phone bill, be nice to the super, find meaningful work, fall in love, get hurt, all of it I resent deeply.

HARRIET. What's the alternative?

JANIE. Dependency. I could marry the pervert who's staring at us. No. That's not a solution. I guess I could always move back to Brookline. Get another Masters in something useful like "Women's Pottery". Do a little freelance writing. Oh God, it's exhausting.

HARRIET. He's coming. (*Marty Sterling enters* D.L. *Janie's mother's dream come true. A prince and a bit of a card.*)

MARTY. Hi.

HARRIET. Hello.

MARTY. You're Harriet Cornwall. I sat behind you during Twentieth Century Problems. I always thought you were a beautiful girl. (*He extends his hand.*) Marty Sterling.

HARRIET. (*Shaking it.*) Hi. And this is Janie Blumberg.

MARTY. Sure. I remember you. I saw you and Harriet together in Cambridge all the time. You always looked more attainable. Frightened to death, but attainable. I'm not attracted to cold people anymore. Who needs that kind of trouble?

HARRIET. I don't know.

MARTY. So what do you do?

JANIE. Oh, I scream here on Central Park South. I'm taking a break now.

HARRIET. Janie and I just moved back to New York together. Well, at the same time. I lived in Italy for a year and Janie was lingering in Brookline, Mass.

MARTY. Good old Brookline. Ever go to Jack and Marian's restaurant? Unbelievable Kasha Varnishka.

HARRIET. Excuse me.

MARTY. Kasha. Little noodle bow ties with barley. Uh, my father's in the restaurant business. Are you familiar with Yee Olde Sterling Tavernes?

HARRIET. Sure. That's a national chain.

MARTY. My father's chain.

HARRIET. (*Impressed.*) Well!

JANIE. Well.

7

MARTY. Well.

JANIE. Well.

HARRIET. Well.

MARTY. Well. I'm on call, I'm a doctor. Kidneys.

HARRIET and JANIE. (*Very impressed.*) Well!

JANIE. Look, maybe you two should sit for a minute, reminisce about Twentieth Century Problems.

MARTY. I wish I could. Good-bye.

HARRIET. Good-bye. (*Marty starts to exit, stops, turns.*)

MARTY. Janie Blumberg. Is your brother Ben Blumberg?

HARRIET. Yup. That's her brother, Ben.

MARTY. I went to Camp Kibbutz with Ben Blumberg when I was nine.

JANIE. Yup, that's my brother, Ben.

MARTY. Would you tell your brother Murray Schlimovitz says hello.

JANIE. Who's Murray Schlimovitz?

MARTY. Me. Before my father owned the Sterling Tavernes, he owned The Schlimovitz Kosher Dairy Restaurants in Brooklyn. But around 15 years ago all the Schlimovitz Restaurants burned down. So for the sake of the family and the business, we changed our names before I entered Harvard. Nice to see you. Bye. (*Marty exits.*)

HARRIET. What were you doing? "Maybe you two should sit and reminisce about Twentieth Century Problems"?

JANIE. Marty Sterling could make a girl a nice husband.

HARRIET. Now you really sound like your mother.

JANIE. Hattie, do you know who that man's father is?

HARRIET. Uh-huh. He's an arsonist.

JANIE. No. He's a genius. Mr. Sterling, the little man who comes on television in a colonial suit and a pilgrim hat to let you know he's giving away free pop-overs and all the shrimp you can eat at Yee Olde Salade and Relish Bar, that guy is Milty Schlimovitz, Marty Sterling's father.

HARRIET. It's all right. I can make do without Doctor Murray Marty and his father's pop-overs. I have to get to that interview. My friend, Joe Stine, the headhunter, says they only have you back if they're going to hire you.

JANIE. Well, if you don't marry Marty Sterling, I'll marry

8

him. Wait till I tell my parents I ran into him. Tasha Blumberg will have the caterers on the other extension.

HARRIET. I'm afraid marrying him isn't a solution. Will you walk me back to Colgate?

JANIE. Sure. If I can get myself up.

HARRIET. Do I look like a successful single woman?

JANIE. Well.

HARRIET. What, well?

JANIE. Hattie, you know the wisdom of Tasha Blumberg?

HARRIET. Which one?

JANIE. Always look nice when you throw out the garbage, you never know who you might meet. Put on your jacket, sweetheart. Always walk with your head up and chest out. Think "I am".

HARRIET. I am. (*Putting on jacket, lifting her head and chest.*)

JANIE. Now I can be seen with you. (*Janie slumps. They exit arm in arm.*)

END SCENE

TELEPHONE MACHINE #2

HARRIET. (*Ring. Beep.*) Janie, I got the job. Sorry I got you up so early. I love you. Bye. (*She sings.*) "School bells ring and children sing, it's back to Robert Hall again." Bye. (*Hang up.*)

JULIE STERN. (*Beep.*) Miss Bloomberg. This is Julie Stern at Woman's Work Magazine. We read your portfolio. Our readers feel you haven't experienced enough women's pain to stimulate our market. Thank you. (*Hang up.*)

CYNTHIA PETERSON. (*Beep.*) Janie, it's Cynthia. There's a Lib/Men, Lib/Women mixer at the Unitarian Church on Friday. It got a four star rating in Wisdom's Child. My cousin, Felice, met an anthropologist there and she's in much worse shape than either of us. Wanna go? (*Hang up.*)

END SCENE

ACT ONE

Scene Two

Janie's apartment. She is asleep on the sofa. Tasha Blumberg enters with an attache case. Tasha is an untraditional Jewish mother with traditional values. She looks over the apartment with disdain. She sets case down on the boxes and sits next to Janie on the sofa.

TASHA. (*Sings and strokes Janie's hair.*) "Is this the little girl I carried. Is this the little boy at play. (*Louder.*) I don't remember growing older, when did they. . . ." (*Janie, waking up, turns and screams.*) Good morning Sweetheart. (*She kisses Janie.*) Congratulations on your new apartment.

JANIE. What?

TASHA. Your father and I came over to celebrate your new apartment. What kind of place is this? There isn't a doorman. Is this place safe for you?

JANIE. Oh Jesus, what are you doing here?

TASHA. I came to celebrate. You know your mother. I like life-life-life. I came over yesterday and you weren't home so I got worried. I had the super give me the key. I thought something happened with the movers.

JANIE. Nothing happened with the movers. Mother, it's seven o'clock in the morning.

TASHA. Isn't that nice. You can have breakfast with me and your father. (*Tasha opens the attache case and turns on an aerobics tape. She starts to warm up.*)

JANIE. What are you doing?

TASHA. I'm warming up for my morning dance class. Why don't you get up and do it with me? If you exercised, you'd have the energy to unpack your crates. (*Tasha continues to exercise.*)

JANIE. Mother, I've only been here two nights. I'll unpack them later.

TASHA. Janie, people who wait, wait. I like go-go. Watch, I'll show you how to do it. (*She does.*) The girls at dancing school admire me so much. They tell me they wish their mothers had so much energy.

10

JANIE. Their mothers probably wear clothes.

TASHA. Why are you so modest?

JANIE. I'm your daughter. I shouldn't be seeing you in tie-dyed underwear.

TASHA. You're making fun of me.

JANIE. I'm not making fun of you.

TASHA. (*Still dancing.*) 1,2,3, hip. 1,2,3, hip.

JANIE. Where's Daddy?

TASHA. I sent him to pick up some coffee.

JANIE. Do the girls at dancing think it's strange you order up breakfast from a coffee shop every morning? (*Tasha turns off music.*)

TASHA. Sweetheart, when you get married, you make breakfast at your house and invite me. Anything you make is fine. You want to make sausages, I'll eat sausages. Do you know what sausages are made of? (*Janie lies back on sofa.*) Janie, please don't lie there like a body. You have everything to look forward to. When you were in high school, the other mothers would stop me on the street and say, "You must be so proud of Janie. She's such a brilliant child. If only my daughters were like Janie."

JANIE. What are the names of these mothers? I want names. (*Doorbell rings.*)

TASHA. There's your father with the coffee. (*Tasha opens front door.*)

SIMON. (*Simon Blumberg, Tasha's partner, a very sweet father though not chatty enters with bag w/coffee & sandwich.*) Janie, is this place safe for you? There isn't a doorman. Why don't you put in the lock I bought you in Brookline?

JANIE. I left it there.

SIMON. You left it in Brookline? That lock cost $50.00.

JANIE. I have it Dad. I have it.

SIMON. You want to split this egg sandwich with me?

TASHA. Simon, please, there's a proper way to do this. First we have to toast Janie's new apartment. (*Tasha hands out the coffees.*) I remember my first apartment in New York. Of course, I was much younger than you and I was married to your father. (*She toasts.*) To Janie. Congratulations, welcome home, and I hope next year you live in another apartment and your father and I have to bring up four coffees.

JANIE. You want me to have a roommate?

TASHA. I want you to be happy. Talk to her Simon like a father and a daughter. Maybe she wants to tell you her problems.

JANIE. I don't have any problems. How's the business, Dad?

SIMON. Your father always with the business right? You want to see something, Janie? (*He pulls out an envelope.*) Smell this.

JANIE. (*Smells the envelope.*) It's nice.

SIMON. I can't make them fast enough. And then those jerks ship me a million envelopes without any perfume. You know what that's going to do to the Valentine season? Your father always with the headaches.

JANIE. It's all right, Dad. I like the envelope. Smells like the state of Maine.

SIMON. You want to come down to the business today and see whether it interests you? Then I'll take you skating after work.

JANIE. I can't Dad. I have to follow up some leads for clients here. Some other time I'd like to. (*Janie puts on a multi-colored sweatshirt over her nightgown.*)

TASHA. Is that an outfit! Simon, from a man's point of view, is that what you'd call an appetizing outfit?

SIMON. If you were a lawyer like your brother, Ben, then it makes sense to go out on your own. But I don't understand why a girl with your intelligence should be freelance writing when you could take over a business.

TASHA. Christ is thinking of going to Law School when the children get a little older.

JANIE. Who?

TASHA. Your sister-in-law, Christ.

JANIE. Chris, mother, it's Chris. I'll come down and see your place next week, Dad. I promise.

SIMON. Take your time, honey. Whenever you're ready.

TASHA. My two big doers. If not today, tomorrow. I can't sit like you two. (*She dances.*) 1,2,3, hip. 1,2,3, hip. (*She goes over to Janie.*)

JANIE. I won't dance. Don't ask me.

TASHA. Look at those thighs. I'm dying. (*She continues dancing.*)

SIMON. What's his name called our house last night looking for you.

TASHA. (*Stops dancing.*) Who? Who?

SIMON. The pop-over boy. He called Ben cause they went to summer camp together. And Ben didn't have your new number so he told him to call us.

JANIE. Ben told Marty Sterling to call you?

TASHA. Please, sweetheart, look nice. It's important. Even when you throw out the garbage. I like this Marty Sterling.

JANIE. You don't even know him.

TASHA. He comes from nice people.

JANIE. His father is an arsonist.

SIMON. Believe me. You can have a nice life with him. Sounds like a very nice boy. He said to give you a message to call him at the hospital. He was in the emergency room at Mount Sinai.

TASHA. I told you he was a nice boy.

JANIE. Don't get too excited. He probably wants Harriet's number.

TASHA. What does Harriet have to do with the pop-over boy?

JANIE. He's her friend.

TASHA. Why do you belittle yourself all the time? What kind of attitude is that? (*Tasha stands.*) Why don't you walk into a room with your head up and your chest out and think, "I am". (*She demonstrates.*) Am I right, Simon?

SIMON. What is it?

TASHA. Sweetheart, stop thinking about those envelopes and look at your daughter. From a man's point of view, isn't that some beautiful face?

JANIE. I am beautiful. People stop each other on the street to say how beautiful I look when I throw out the garbage. And when Marty Sterling proposes, he'll say, "Janie Jill Blumberg, I want to spend the rest of my life with you because every member of your family calls me the pop-over boy and I want to be near your mother in her tie-dyed underwear."

TASHA. She's making fun of me again.

JANIE. I'm not making fun of you. It's good to be home. (*The three kiss.*) If I was still in Brookline, what time is it? 7:15. If I was still in Brookline, I'd be sleeping. Here by 7:15, there's a catered meal and a floor show.

TASHA. The girls at dancing say you can always have a good time with Tasha. Honey, it's wonderful to see you. Thank you for having us, I loved your cooking, and I'm sure you'd like me to stay and chat all day but your father isn't the only one who has to get to work. I'm demonstrating in class today.

SIMON. Have a nice day, Janie. (*He kisses Janie and starts to exit.*)

TASHA. Where are you going? Give her some money so she'll buy a lock.

SIMON. (*Giving Janie some bills.*) Honey, I'm sorry if I seem preoccupied. Mother walks me to work every morning now. Once I walk a few blocks, my mind gets stimulated. You know, Janie, I used to have the same trouble with my legs as you do. I would have to sit in bed and rest all the time. But you know what makes the difference? Ripple soles. You get a pair of shoes like these and then you're in business. (*He gives Janie more bills.*)

JANIE. Thanks Daddy.

TASHA. So you'll call this Marty Sterling?

JANIE. (*Pats Tasha's head.*) I will call him. I will call him.

TASHA. Am I getting shorter? I'm getting shorter.

JANIE. You're fine mother. (*Janie flops back onto sofa.*)

TASHA. Body, please, don't get back into the bed. You have everything ahead of you. You can have a family, you can have a career, and you can learn to tap dance.

JANIE. Are you taking tap dancing?

TASHA. It's part of life. I'll teach you. (*She taps quite smoothly, calling out the steps, "flap, heel, flap, touch," and ends in a "Ta-da" pose.*)

SIMON. (*While Tasha dances.*) I told your mother she could run her own dancing school.

TASHA. (*Ends dance.*) Two lessons.

SIMON. Don't you think your mother looks nice? That's a new attache.

TASHA. I'm an executive mother.

JANIE. It looks very nice.

TASHA. You want it?

JANIE. You keep it mother.

SIMON. Let's go dear. (*Tasha starts to go.*)

Remember. Ripple soles. (*He exits. Janie flops back on sofa.*)

JANIE. Oy!

TASHA. Janie, please, only old ladies sigh. Oy! (*She exits.*)

END SCENE

14

ACT ONE

Scene Three

Lillian Cornwall's Office. Lillian Cornwall, an impressive, handsome woman, whose demeanor commands respect, is seated behind her desk. She is speaking on the phone.

LILLIAN. Obviously Dick, our only choice is to go national with this. I don't care what some kid in your department says about numbers. Hold on a minute, will you. (*She pushes a button on the phone.*) Lillian Cornwall. (*She yells off stage.*) Pauline, no one's picking up the phone here. (*She hits another button.*) Dick, trust me on this one. I'm not being too harsh. No, I didn't think so. Thank you. (*She hits another button.*) Lillian Cornwall's office. (*She yells off stage.*) Pauline! (*Back on the phone.*) I'm sorry, Mrs. Cornwall isn't in, can I take a message? Oh Dick, it's you. Well, tell the kid in your department I appreciate his confidence. What can I say? I'm a beautiful, successful, brilliant woman. Dick, I'm simply not a kid. (*Phone buzzes.*) Hold a sec, would you? (*She pushes another button.*) Yes, Pauline. (*She pushes another button.*) Dick, my lovely daughter is here. Gotta go. (*She hangs up. Harriet enters in a stylish business suit. She is carrying a gift box.*)
HARRIET. Hello mother.
LILLIAN. Hello, baby, it's nice to see you. (*They kiss.*)
HARRIET. You're looking well.
LILLIAN. What brings you here? Would you like me to order you a salad or some lunch? I'd call Tom and get us into the Four Seasons, but I have a meeting in a few minutes.
HARRIET. That's all right. I have to get back to the office. Ummmm. (*Harriet takes out three noisemakers and blows them, handing Lillian the present.*) Happy Birthday Mother!
LILLIAN. Hmmmm?
HARRIET. Happy Birthday. I bought this for you in Italy before I ran out of money.
LILLIAN. Oh God, I bet that meeting is a birthday thing. Thank you, Harriet, it's very handsome. (*She puts gift back in box.*) How are things at Colgate?
HARRIET. Fine.
LILLIAN. Don't say fine, Harriet. You're a Harvard M.B.A. I expect an analysis.

15

HARRIET. We're changing the test market from Sacramento to Syracuse.

LILLIAN. Makes sense. And your personal life?

HARRIET. Mother!

LILLIAN. I don't have much time to catch up. I have a meeting.

HARRIET. My personal life is O.K.

LILLIAN. Is that better or worse than fine?

HARRIET. It's O.K. Janie's back in New York and that's nice. I see my friend from Harvard, Joe Stine, the headhunter.

LILLIAN. Nice boy.

HARRIET. Nice. A little dull.

LILLIAN. Sweet though. No you're right. A little dull.

HARRIET. And I'm sort of interested in some guy in my office.

LILLIAN. Is that a good idea?

HARRIET. I'm not seeing him. I'm just attracted to him.

LILLIAN. Sounds like a pleasant arrangement. What does he do?

HARRIET. Mother!

LILLIAN. His job, baby, what does he do?

HARRIET. He does all right. He's my boss's boss.

LILLIAN. How old is he?

HARRIET. Around forty.

LILLIAN. Around forty? He should be further along than your boss's boss.

HARRIET. Happy Birthday mother.

LILLIAN. Harriet, you can ask me questions about my life right after I'm finished with yours. You're not making this easy, baby.

HARRIET. Sometimes you're hard to take, mother.

LILLIAN. So they say. (*Intercom buzz, Lillian answers.*) Bill, I'll be there in a minute. My daughter is with me. Can she be present at this meeting. I thought so. Thanks Bill. (*She hangs up.*) It is a birthday thing. Harriet, why don't you come with me? You can be my date.

HARRIET. Mother, do you remember when you would take me to Group Sales Meetings in Barbados? And I would appear in Mary Janes as your date at candle lit dinners by the ocean.

LILLIAN. You were a wonderful date. Interesting, attractive, bright. Certainly more suitable than what was available.

HARRIET. Mother, you're so crazy. I hope I'm going to be all right.

LILLIAN. You'll be fine. Don't dwell on it. Your generation is absolutely fascinated with itself. Think about science? Technology is going to change our world significantly. So, do you want to come?

HARRIET. Sure.

LILLIAN. God, I dread going to these kinds of things.

HARRIET. Me too.

LILLIAN. I'm not being too harsh?

HARRIET. No, you're not being too harsh.

LILLIAN. Comb your hair, baby. I like it better off your face.

END SCENE

ACT ONE

Scene Four

Italian Restaurant. Marty and Janie seated.

MARTY. Do you want dessert? Because if you don't like the dessert here, my father is giving away free pop-overs in the Paramus Mall. So what do you think you're going to do now?

JANIE. With my life? At this restaurant? Tonight?

MARTY. Now that you've come home.

JANIE. I don't know. Retire. I sent away for some brochures from Heritage Village.

MARTY. I think about retirement. Not that I don't like being a doctor, but I don't want to get trapped. You know what I mean? First, you get the cuisinart, then the bigger apartment, and then the Mercedes, and the next thing you know, you're charging $250 to Mrs. Feldman, with the rash, to tell her, "Mrs. Feldman, you have a rash".

JANIE. Whenever I get most depressed, I think I should take charge of my life and apply to medical school. Then I remember that I once identified a liver as a heart. Really, I demonstrated the right auricle and the left ventricle on this liver.

17

MARTY. I left medical school after my first year to do carpentry for a year.

JANIE. Your father must have liked that.

MARTY. He wants me to be happy. I'm very close to my parents.

JANIE. That's nice. (*Pause.*) I'm sorry. I was thinking about my parents.

MARTY. Are you close to them?

JANIE. In a way. She's a dancer and he's very sweet. It's complicated.

MARTY. My father started out in show business. He used to tell jokes at Grossingers. That's why he does the pop-over commercials himself. Now he's the Toastmaster General for the United Jewish Appeal.

JANIE. Have you ever been to Israel?

MARTY. I worked on a Kibbutz the second time I dropped out of medical school. Israel's very important to me. In fact, I have to decide next month if I want to open my practice here in New York or Tel Aviv.

JANIE. Oh.

MARTY. Why, are you anti-Israel?

JANIE. No. Of course not. I preferred the people my parent's age there to the younger ones. The people my age intimidated me. I'd be sleeping and they'd go off to turn deserts into forests. The older ones had more humanity. They rested sometimes.

MARTY. I think Jewish families should have at least three children.

JANIE. Excuse me?

MARTY. It's a dying religion. Intermarriage, Ivy League Colleges, the New York Review of Books. (*Pause.*) So, how's Harriet?

JANIE. She's fine.

MARTY. She's not sweet like you.

JANIE. Harriet is wonderful.

MARTY. She's like those medical school girls. They're nice but they'd bite your balls off. You think Israelis have no sense of humor. Believe me, women medical students are worse. (*He takes Janie's hand.*) Janie, you're one of the few real people I've ever met in a long time. Most of the women I meet aren't funny.

18

JANIE. (*Quickly.*) Marty, I think I should tell you I find the fact that you don't like women doctors extremely disturbing and discriminatory. I support the concept of Israel and would probably be a much happier, healthier person if I could go out into the desert and build a forest, but I am far too lazy and self-involved. I have very fat thighs and I want very badly to be someone else without going through the effort of actually changing myself into someone else. I have very little courage but I'm highly critical of others who don't.

MARTY. (*Sweetly.*) Is that it?

JANIE. And I want you to like me very much.

MARTY. Do you like me?

JANIE. Yes.

MARTY. Sounds tentative. Most women fall in love the minute they hear "Volare". Maybe this will help. I bought it for you when I was in Rome. (*He hands Janie a swizzle stick.*)

JANIE. I was wondering why they have swizzle sticks in the wine.

MARTY. (*A la the Godfather.*) I got connections in the restaurant business. (*Marty takes Janie's hand.*) Should I take you home, Monkey?

JANIE. What?

MARTY. Want to go home?

JANIE. No. My interior decorator is there.

MARTY. Want to come to my parents house? They should be out late tonight. After Paramus, there's a UJA testimonial dinner for my father. It means a lot to him cause he's been giving away so much shrimp at the salad bar, they almost revoked his job as Toastmaster.

JANIE. It's weird going to someone's parent's house. Shouldn't we have mortgages and children?

MARTY. Let's go, Monkey. You'll be all right. I'll help you.

JANIE. (*Rises.*) And what'll I do for you?

MARTY. (*Rises.*) Be sweet. I need attention. A great deal of attention. (*As lights fade, Janie puts her head on Marty's shoulder.*)

END SCENE

ACT ONE

Scene Five

Harriet's apartment. Harriet and Paul Stuart enter. Paul is about 40. He is very corporate and appealing looking. Harriet takes both their coats and tosses them on the chair. She exits into the kitchen. Paul moves to sofa, takes out Binaca, gives himself a hit and sits. Harriet enters pushing a rolling bar. She crosses down to S.R. of sofa, stops and poses.

PAUL. You remind me a lot of my first wife.

HARRIET. Mr. Stuart, would you like something to drink? I don't have much. I just moved here.

PAUL. Scotch on the rocks. My first wife hated office Christmas parties.

HARRIET. I'm sorry. Did I make you leave?

PAUL. Definitely not. You're one of the most amusing people I've met at Colgate in a long time. Can I tell you something as a friend? You don't have to call me Mr. Stuart.

HARRIET. I think it's funny your name is Paul Stuart. If your name was Brooks Brothers, I'd call you Mr. Brothers. (*She hands him napkin with cracker and plate.*) Pate?

PAUL. (*He takes it.*) Where are you from originally? (*Paul cracks up.*) Have you ever noticed when you try a conversation opener like, "Where are you from originally?", you always sound like a jerk?

HARRIET. I grew up in New York. My mother still lives on East 69th Street.

PAUL. East 69th Street. You were a rich kid.

HARRIET. No. Upper middle class.

PAUL. Only rich kids know what upper middle class is.

HARRIET. Well, I wasn't spoiled. Definitely not spoiled.

PAUL. Your father was a lawyer?

HARRIET. No. My mother's an executive.

PAUL. Is your mother Lillian Cornwall?

HARRIET. Yup.

PAUL. Jesus. I interviewed with your mother once. That women has balls. Do you know what it took for a woman at her time to get as far as she did?

20

HARRIET. Yup.

PAUL. Poor baby, I bet you do. (*He lights her cigarette.*) Would you like me to spoil you a bit? Relax. For a girl with such a good mind, you get tense too easily. (*They both start laughing.*) Why are you laughing?

HARRIET. You're amazing. First you tell me how amusing I am, then you want to spoil me and now you tell me what a good mind I have. What are you going to do next? Ask me to come up and see your etchings? (*Paul moves away to his drink.*) I'm sorry. This is making me a little uncomfortable. Office romance and all that. You're my boss's boss.

PAUL. Harriet, do you know that 40% of the people at McKinsey are having inter office affairs?

HARRIET. How do you know that?

PAUL. Friend of mine did the study. Look, I live with a woman so no one will know. Is that an incentive?

HARRIET. (*Rises.*) Cathy? Do you live with Cathy?

PAUL. How do you know Cathy?

HARRIET. She calls the office three times a day.

PAUL. (*Rises.*) You've been paying attention.

HARRIET. I'm a smart kid.

PAUL. (*Grabbing Harriet's ass.*) Smart woman.

HARRIET. (*Pulling away.*) Paul, I generally try not to get involved with unavailable men.

PAUL. You've never been with a married man? How old are you? (*Paul chokes.*)

HARRIET. Are you all right?

PAUL. Jesus, were there any nuts in that pate? My doctor told me not to eat nuts. I've got this stomach thing. I tell you, when you get older, you really gotta watch it. But you'll take good care of me, right Beauty? (*Pause.*) Are you excited?

HARRIET. Where are you from originally?

PAUL. You're excited. Don't be embarrassed, Beauty. I'll be wonderful for you Harriet. You'll try to change me, you'll realize you can't and furthermore, I'm not worth it, so you'll marry some nice investment banker and make your mother happy.

HARRIET. I don't think my mother particularly wants me to get married. I don't particularly want me to get married.

PAUL. You'll change your mind. Career girls, when they hit

21

thirty, all change their minds. Look, whatever is happening here, we better do it quickly because Cathy is expecting me home with the laundry at 11:00. I'm very attracted to you, Harriet.

HARRIET. 40% of the people at McKinsey, huh?

PAUL. And those are just the ones crazy enough to fill out the questionnaire.

HARRIET. Get out of here.

PAUL. C'mere. Deal from strength, Harriet. Men really like strong women.

END SCENE

ACT ONE

Scene Six

Janie in her apartment, typing. Doorbell rings, Janie opens door. Harriet enters with package.

HARRIET. Congratulations on your new apartment!

JANIE. Harriet, I've been living here three months.

HARRIET. That's why I came to celebrate. I decided this morning it was time for you to unpack. Did I walk in with my right foot first?

JANIE. I don't know.

HARRIET. Then I have to do it again. (*She exits. Doorbell rings. Janie opens door and Harriet re-enters.*) Congratulations on your new apartment!

JANIE. What are you doing?

HARRIET. I looked all this up very carefully in the Oxford Companion to Jewish life.

JANIE. I'm not familiar with this companion.

HARRIET. You have to walk into a new apartment with your right foot to set you off on the right foot. Here, I also brought you a house warming gift. But you cannot open it til we get you settled in.

JANIE. Harriet, you know I can't postpone, gratification.

HARRIET. Janie, you have to make a home for yourself.

22

Now, what are we going to do with these crates? (*Harriet picks up crates.*)

JANIE. Harriet, what are you doing? You're flying around the room.

HARRIET. (*Exiting with crates.*) It's Saturday.

JANIE. The day of rest. Didn't they tell you that in the Oxford Companion?

HARRIET. (*Enters empty handed.*) It's Paul Stuart's day at home with Cathy. You want me to put the typewriter in the bedroom? (*She picks up typewriter.*)

JANIE. (*Stops her.*) No, I'm working. Marty's father hired an actor to play a popover at the opening of the New Sterling Tavern in the Green Acres Mall and Marty got me a job writing the pop-over's opening remarks. Hattie, don't you mind not seeing Paul on the weekend?

HARRIET. No, it's O.K. As I see it, Paul Stuart is fine until I find the right relationship. It's similar to the case method. And he's great in bed. (*Harriet sets down typewriter.*)

JANIE. Marty claims he slept with over 100 visiting nurses when he was at Harvard.

HARRIET. (*Sits.*) Really!?

JANIE. I just told you that so you'd sit down. (*Janie sits.*)

HARRIET. So, is it something with Marty?

JANIE. He decided to open his practice here next month and he's invited me to his parent's house for Chanukah. Somedays I walk down the street and think if I don't step on any cracks, I'll marry Marty. What ever happened to Janie Blumberg? She did so well, she married Marty the doctor. They're giving away pop-overs in Paramus. (*Pause.*) Hattie, do you think I should marry Marty?

HARRIET. I've always hated women who sit around talking about how there are no men in New York. Or everyone is gay or married.

JANIE. What does this have to do with my marrying Marty?

HARRIET. These women would tell you, "Marry him. He's straight, he'll make a nice living, he'll be a good father." Janie, what women like Cynthia Peterson don't know is, no matter how lonely you get or how many birth announcements you receive, the trick is not to get frightened. There's nothing wrong with being alone.

23

JANIE. Harriet, do you remember when we would listen to "My Guy" and iron our hair before going to a High School dance?

HARRIET. Oh God, I've blocked all of that.

JANIE. I remember arriving at the dance, looking over the prospects and thinking when I'm 28, I'm going to get married and be very much in love with someone who is poor and fascinating until he's 30 and then fabulously wealthy and very secure after that. And we're going to have children who wear overalls and flannel shirts and are kind and independent with curly blond hair. And we'll have great sex and still hold hands when we travel to China when we're sixty.

HARRIET. I never thought about any of that. Maybe it's cause I'm Lillian's daughter, but I never respected women who didn't learn to live alone and pay their own rent. Imagine spending your life pretending you weren't a person. To compromise at this point would be anti-feminist, well, anti-humanist, well, just not impressive. I'm not being too harsh.

JANIE. No. Just rhetorical. (*Doorbell rings.*)

HARRIET. Who's that?

JANIE. I don't know. (*Janie answers door. Vladimir around 30, a Russian taxi cab driver, very impressed with capitalism is there, holding a bar. The bar has a safari motif.*)

VLADIMIR. Hello hi.

JANIE. Do you have the right apartment?

VLADIMIR. You are Miss Blumberg?

JANIE. Yes.

VLADIMIR. For you. I am Vladimir. I am filmmaker from Moscow. I drive taxi now. (*He enters with bar. He sees Harriet.*) Hello. Hi.

SIMON. (*Enters with stool.*) Janie, do you like this bar? Hello, Harriet. We thought you might need something to entertain at home.

TASHA. (*Enters with stool.*) Don't force her Simon. Hello darling. (*Notices Harriet.*) Harriet, you look terrific. Are you seeing anyone?

HARRIET. Sort of.

SIMON. We met Vladimir on the cab ride down here. He came from Moscow six weeks ago.

JANIE. That's nice. Do you like it here?

VLADIMIR. Hello hi.

SIMON. He doesn't speak very much English.

TASHA. That doesn't matter. If you like people you speak every language. I can get along in any country. If you smile, you dance, anyone will understand.

JANIE. My mother identifies with Zorba the Greek.

VLADIMIR. Zorba. Yes. Thank you.

TASHA. Harriet, do you like the bar? I saw another one but I was afraid Janie would say it's too old, it's too new, it's gold.

HARRIET. I like it very much. It's primitive.

SIMON. Vladimir, maybe you want to stay and put the bar together and Mrs. Blumberg and Harriet and I can bring you up some coffee.

VLADIMIR. Coffee. Regular.

TASHA. Sit. Harriet, join us. Harriet's with Colgate Palmolive.

SIMON. (*Takes Janie aside.*) He's a nice boy. Don't you think he's a nice boy, Janie? Seems intelligent too. I thought maybe if things didn't work out with you and Marty, I'd take him into the business.

JANIE. You're kidding. This man is here six weeks and he gets a wife, a business, and a dancing mother-in-law.

SIMON. What's wrong with giving a guy a break?

JANIE. (*Making a sign to get Vladimir out.*) Dad. . . .

SIMON. Vladimir. Thank you. We'll take the taxi uptown to Rockefeller Center.

TASHA. Every Saturday I take Mr. Blumberg skating.

SIMON. My partner keeps me in shape.

TASHA. Harriet, you look terrific. Who is it you're seeing?

JANIE. She's seeing someone who's married.

TASHA. Let's go dear. (*Tasha & Simon exit.*)

HARRIET & JANIE. Good-bye. Good-bye. Nice to see you.

VLADIMIR. (*To Harriet.*) Good-bye. (*To Janie.*) Good-bye. (*He exits.*)

JANIE. One of these days, I'm going to write a book, *My Mother Herself.* I'm sorry, Hattie. That was the only way I could get them out of here.

HARRIET. (*Looking at Bar.*) Did Tasha go on safari?

JANIE. No, she went hunting at K-Mart. Harriet, they brought over a Russian taxi cab driver for me to marry! Maybe I should move back to Brookline tomorrow.

25

HARRIET. You can't leave me here with Lillian and Paul Stuart. I brought Lillian a birthday present that I bought with my last lire in Italy. She hardly opened it. She couldn't wait to get back to the intercom to harass Pauline. Janie, sit, it's the day of rest. Now you can open your present. (*Harriet brings her the bag and they sit on the sofa. Janie puts the bow on her head and takes out a loaf of Hallah bread, a box of kosher salt, sugar, matches and a candle.*)

JANIE. What kind of diet are you on?

HARRIET. According to the Oxford Companion, this is what your family brings when you move into a new home. Bread — the staple of life. Sugar — something sweet in your life. Salt — a little spice in your life.

JANIE. I have that.

HARRIET. And a candle to light the way. (*She lights candle.*) Janie, you know what I remember more than those mixers?

JANIE. What? (*She puts her arm on Harriet's shoulder.*)

HARRIET. Remember when you and I would meet for dinner cause Lil was at a meeting and Tasha only had Brewers Yeast in the refrigerator. I always thought, well, I do have a family. Janie's my family. In fact, that still helps a lot. I always assumed it was some sort of pact.

JANIE. It is a pact. (*Both girls break off a piece of bread from the loaf.*) Hattie, thank you for my gift from my family. (*She picks up salt.*) Cheers.

HARRIET. (*Picks up sugar.*) Le Chaim. (*They clink the boxes.*)

END SCENE

TELEPHONE MACHINE #3

HART FARRELL. (*Beep.*) Janie Blumberg. This is Hart Farrell in the personnel department at Sesame Street. A temp in our office recognized your name from a part he played in the Green Acres Mall. I heard your pieces. I'm going to pass them on to Tajlei Kaplan Singleberry. Nice song Luv. (*Phone hangs up.*)

CYNTHIA PETERSON. (*Beep. Crying.*) Janie, it's Cynthia. Thank God you have your machine on. I'm home, I'm broke, my trainer is on retreat, I've been rejected by every man on the

Upper West Side and I'm about to get drunk. Janie, do you know a good dry cleaner?

END SCENE

ACT ONE

SCENE SEVEN

Janie's apartment, L. *Sofa and TV on a box. Harriet's living room/bedroom,* R. *Foldout bed, ottoman, TV. Paul & Harriet in bed. Light up on Janie's apartment.*

JANIE. (*Entering.*) I fucked up Chanukah.

MARTY. (*Entering.*) You were sweet.

JANIE. I'm sorry I spilled horseradish on your sister-in-law. They have a nice baby. Really, Schlomo is very sweet. I'm sorry I spilled horseradish on Schlomo. (*She exits into bedroom.*)

MARTY. You worry too much. You're just like my mother. My mother says you're shy and a little clumsy because you're very angry with your family. But she says don't worry you'll grow out of it. I told her your mother was a bit cuckoo.

JANIE. (*Entering.*) Martin, I'm reflective and eager to please and my mother is a pioneer in interpretive dance. (*She exits into bedroom.*)

MARTY. Don't be so defensive, sweetheart.

JANIE. (*Offstage.*) Everything by you is so simple.

MARTY. Everything by you is harder than it has to be. You think my sister-in-law knew what she was doing when she married my brother? (*Janie enters. She has changed from her dress into sweatshirt and overalls.*) That didn't come out right, did it?

JANIE. That's O.K.

MARTY. You know what I mean. My sister-in-law had even less direction than you do and she's a bright girl too. But she met my brother and now she's a wonderful mother, and believe me, when Schlomo is a little older, she'll go back to work in something nice — she'll teach or she'll work with the elderly — and she won't conquer the world, but she'll have a nice life. (*Pause.*) Monkey, I don't want to be alone. But I think it's

27

going to be all right with us. I love you. (*Pause.*) I put a deposit down on an apartment for us in Brooklyn today.

JANIE. What?

MARTY. I figured if I waited for you to make up your mind to move, we'd never take anything and I need a place to live before I open my practice. You don't have to pay your half of the deposit now. I can wait a month. Is that okay?

JANIE. Sure.

MARTY. I decided we should live in Flatbush or Brighton Beach where people have real values. My father never sees those people anymore, the Alta Kakas in Brooklyn, the old men with the accents who sit in front of Hymie's Highway Delicatessen. I miss them. My father never goes to Miami anymore. They go to Palm Springs or Martinique with their friends from The Westchester Country Club. My father thought my brother was crazy when he named his son, Schlomo. He kept asking my brother, "So what's his real name?" And my father will think I'm crazy when we move to Brooklyn.

JANIE. Marty?

MARTY. What is it, Monkey? Are you angry?

JANIE. No. I like the Alta Kakas in Brooklyn, too. I always thought Herman Wouk should write a novel, *Young Kaka.* I don't know.

MARTY. What don't you know? Janie, you're 28 years old. What I'm saying is either you want to be with me, you don't have to, you should just want to, and if you don't want to, then we should just forget it.

JANIE. I want to.

MARTY. So, what's the problem?

JANIE. No problem.

MARTY. Uh-oh. What time is it? I promised my father we'd watch his new commercial. (*Marty turns on the TV. Paul turns on their TV at the same time.*)

HARRIET. I know that man.

VOICEOVER. (*Captain Milty Sterling.*) This is Captain Milty Sterling. I'm here at the beautiful Green Acres Mall with the Pop-Over Boy and my grandson, Schlomo. What are we giving away today, Schlomo?

VOICEOVER. (*Schlomo.*) We're giving away shrimp. We're

giving away lobster tails. We're giving away cole slaw.

VOICEOVER. (*Milty.*) How do you like that shrimp, Schlomo?

VOICEOVER. (*Schlomo.*) It's good grandpa.

VOICEOVER. (*Announcer.*) Sterling Taverns now located in Green Acres, Syosset, Paramus, Albany, Plattsburg, Marine Park, Midwood, Madison, Bethesda, and The Bergen Mall. (*Lights fade on Marty & Janie and come up on Paul & Harriet.*)

PAUL. Why are you laughing? The man's a marketing genius. He's giving away shrimp. He's giving away cole slaw. I never heard of such an incentive program. How much do you think he can give away and still make a profit? (*Paul hugs Harriet.*) It's good grandpa. (*Paul gets up.*)

HARRIET. Where are you going?

PAUL. It's late.

HARRIET. You could spend the night.

PAUL. Cathy.

HARRIET. Do you love Cathy?

PAUL. She's devoted to me.

HARRIET. Does Cathy exist?

PAUL. Of course Cathy exists.

HARRIET. I thought maybe Cathy was an answering service you hired to call you three times a day.

PAUL. (*Sitting back on the bed.*) Did I tell you to deal from strength?

HARRIET. Yes.

PAUL. Sometimes I'm a jackass. You're sweet, Harriet. You know that? You're a sweet woman. A lot of people never get off in their entire life. Do you think your mother's had good sex?

HARRIET. My mother likes to watch The Rockford File reruns at 11:00. (*Harriet gets out of bed.*) Paul, I don't think people spend as much time thinking about sex as you do.

PAUL. (*Following her.*) Tell me what you like, Beauty.

HARRIET. The other day I was standing in front of your office with my pert charts and you called your secretary "Beauty", you called whoever called you on the phone "Beauty", and I think you called the ninety year old messenger boy from Ogilvy and Mather "Beauty".

PAUL. I see what's going on here. It's the old, "I'm afraid of turning thirty alone and I'm beginning to think about having a family".

29

HARRIET. Wanting two nights a week or a sleep over date isn't quite a family.

PAUL. Baby, I'm older than you. I've been through this with a lot of women. You want a man who sees you as a potential mother but also is someone who isn't threatened by your success and is deeply interested in it. And this man should be thought of as "intelligent" by your friends, but when you need him, he should drop whatever it is he's doing and be supportive.

HARRIET. I'm not asking for that. Why are you so bitter?

PAUL. Don't be naive. Everything is a negotiation, Harriet. Everything. When I graduated from Yale, I thought I'd find a nice wife who would cook me dinner, we'd have a few kids and I'd support the family, and a few years up we'd get a house in Madison, Connecticut for the weekends. The girl I married never cooked and she wasn't lucky like you. Girls didn't assume they'd have careers then. My wife was just very bright and very unhappy. And the girls I date now, the ones like you, the M.B.A.'s from Harvard, they want me to be the wife. They want me to be the support system. Well, I can't do that. Harriet, I just wasn't told that's the way it was supposed to be.

HARRIET. Paul, I never knew which way it was supposed to be.

PAUL. What do you mean?

HARRIET. I don't really expect anything from you.

PAUL. You and I are a lot alike, Harriet. We don't want to be alone and we don't want to move forward. So we serve a perfect function blocking each other's lives.

HARRIET. I like you, Paul.

PAUL. My poor baby. (*They kiss and get back onto the bed as the lights fade down on them and up on Janie and Marty.*)

MARTY. I'm hungry. What do you have to eat, Monkey?

JANIE. We could order up a sandwich. I have the phone number of every coffee shop on the Upper East and West Side — Four Brothers, The Four Brothers On The Acropolis, The Four Brothers On The Parthenon, The Four Brothers. . . .

MARTY. I'll go to the supermarket, get some chicken and some lettuce and stuff.

JANIE. No. No. No. We can order up a salad.

MARTY. Monkey, you don't know how to cook a chicken?

JANIE. I do. I do. I do. I can make teflon chicken.

MARTY. You shouldn't put yourself down like that. (*Marty gets up to go.*)
JANIE. Marty. I love you. We can take the place in Brooklyn. I just want to be with you. (*Marty comes back and kisses Janie, crosses to front door and exits triumphantly. Janie goes to phone and dials. Phone rings in Harriet's apartment. Harriet picks up.*)
HARRIET. Hello.
JANIE. Hattie, how do you cook a chicken? Marty's coming back here in five minutes with a chicken.
HARRIET. Do you want Florentine or something nice?
JANIE. Hattie, hurry. I can't tell him I don't know how. Marty took an apartment for us in Brooklyn and I can't tell him we have to order up chicken.
HARRIET. Why Brooklyn?
JANIE. He likes Hymie of Hymie's Highway Delicatessen.
HARRIET. Excuse me?
JANIE. He likes the Alta Kakas. (*Janie's doorbell rings.*)
JANIE. Marty, just a sec. Hattie, how do you cook a chicken?
PAUL. (*Getting up.*) Beauty, do you have any Di-gel?
HARRIET. In the cabinet. (*Janie crosses to door.*) Janie, what are altered Kakas? (*Janie opens door. Vladimir is there.*)
VLADIMIR. Hello. Hi. I am in neighborhood. So I drop in. Want to see The Sorrow And The Pity?
JANIE. (*Back on phone.*) Hattie, I have to go. Vladimir is here. He wants to see The Sorrow And The Pity. When can I see you?
HARRIET. I don't know. I don't have my book here. (*Janie's doorbell rings.*)
PAUL. What's wrong with this mouthwash?
HARRIET. It's a Colgate product. (*Vladimir answers door. Simon enters with coffee table.*)
SIMON. Oh hello, Vladimir. How are you?
VLADIMIR. Fine. Thank-you. How's it going?
SIMON. Janie, I brought over a coffee table.
PAUL. I better go, Beauty. Cathy.
HARRIET. Me too. The Rockford Files. (*Marty enters with a bag of groceries. Paul & Harriet engage in a long kiss.*)
MARTY. Monkey, I got the chicken.
JANIE. Marty, this is my father, Simon Blumberg, and Vladimir.

SIMON. Very nice to meet you. Mrs. Blumberg will be so sorry she missed you.

JANIE. (*Into phone.*) Harriet!

VLADIMIR. Hello-hi.

SIMON. Vladimir is my friend. Janie doesn't even *know* him. He's a filmmaker from Moscow. Let's go, Vladimir. (*Simon starts pulling Vladimir out the door.*) Nice to meet you. My best to your family.

PAUL. (*At Harriet's front door.*) I think we have a pretty good thing going. Think about it. (*Paul exits and Simon & Vladimir exit simultaneously.*)

HARRIET. (*On phone.*) Janie!

MARTY. Who's the filmmaker?

JANIE. Friend of my father's.

MARTY. I'm hungry. Are you sure you can cook a chicken? (*Marty hands Janie a chicken wrapped in butcher paper.*) I'll go warm up the oven.

JANIE. I'll get the stapler. (*Marty exits into the kitchen. Janie, back on phone.*) Hattie!

HARRIET. Janie, you never mentioned an apartment. When did you see it?

JANIE. I haven't seen it. Marty told me about it tonight after I spilled horseradish on baby Schlomo.

HARRIET. Janie, people named Homo and Schlymie. I feel our move back to New York has been very successful. I've met a sadist vice president and you've become involved in a shtetl.

MARTY. (*Offstage.*) Monkey!

JANIE. Be right there, Marty. Hattie, how do you cook a chicken?

HARRIET. You just put it in the broiler.

JANIE. Who told you this? Thank you, Harriet. Bye. (*She hangs up.*)

HARRIET. Bye, Janie. (*She hangs up. Janie unwraps the chicken on the coffee table. She lifts it up by the two wings, over her head. She stares at it.*)

PAUL. (*Enters.*) Beauty, Thursday the laundry's open til midnight.

MARTY. (*Enters.*) Janie, the oven's ready. (*Both Janie and Harriet cross up together to Marty & Paul respectively as the lights fade. Janie is cradling the chicken like a baby and Harriet is carried off by Paul. Both* *couples kiss as they exit. We hear a string version of "Isn't It Romantic."**)

END OF ACT ONE

*See Special Note on copyright page.

ACT TWO

Scene One

Central Park South. Tasha enters wearing earphones connected to a walkman tape recorder in her attache case. She is listening to music that makes her dance as she walks. She sits on bench, opens attache case and wipes her face with a towel. Lillian enters, eating a hot dog, and sees Tasha.

LILLIAN. Mrs. Blumberg. (*Tasha doesn't hear her.*) Mrs. Blumberg!

TASHA. (*Loudly.*) Yes.

LILLIAN. Lillian Cornwall.

TASHA. (*Removing her earphones.*) How are you? Please excuse my appearance. I just got out of class. A real workout I had today.

LILLIAN. You look marvelous. How's Ben?

TASHA. Ben is doing very well. He's a lawyer with Korvettes. I mean Cravath.

LILLIAN. And Simon?

TASHA. Simon is with his business. He would love for Janie to take over but Janie says she's happy freelance writing.

LILLIAN. I always liked Janie. She's such a bright girl.

TASHA. (*Right again.*) I tell her people stop me on the street to tell me how bright she is, but she doesn't believe me. Janie tells me Harriet has a nice job.

LILLIAN. Yes. She's at Colgate Palmolive.

TASHA. She's going to be an executive mother like you. Very nice. Do you see the girls much? My daughter, whenever I call her, I get the machine.

LILLIAN. I reach Harriet's secretary or rather my secretary reaches Harriet's secretary.

TASHA. She's always been a hard worker, your Harriet.

LILLIAN. Harriet tells me Janie's been seeing a nice boy.

TASHA. He's a very nice boy. But so what? Harriet and Janie are very nice girls. They deserve a little "naches". You know what I mean by "naches"? A little happiness. Well, I don't want to keep you. I know you're a busy woman. You probably have appointments.

34

LILLIAN. Actually, I thought I'd surprise Harriet and take her to a nice lunch, but her secretary told me she was in a meeting. So I thought I'd treat myself to a frankfurter in the park. I haven't had a frankfurter in the park since I lived in England, thirty years ago.

TASHA. Can I tell you something? I'm sorry, I forgot your first name.

LILLIAN. Lillian

TASHA. Lillian, maybe it's none of my business, but you shouldn't eat frankfurters. You know what frankfurters are made of? Have some string beans. (*She takes out bag of string beans from attache case.*) All the young girls at dancing school carry plastic bags with string beans.

LILLIAN. (*Taking a bean.*) Thank you.

TASHA. (*Sits and sighs.*) Excuse me, I always tell my daughter only old ladies sigh. My husband has an expression, "everything presses itself out". Believe me, Harriet will find a nice boy, she'll get married, she'll work, she'll have a nice life. I don't understand why they're fighting it so hard.

LILLIAN. I don't think Harriet thinks about marriage very much.

TASHA. These days they "live together". That's the latest. Believe me, it's the same thing as being married.

LILLIAN. Harriet told me she doesn't particularly want to live with anyone. I don't live with anyone.

TASHA. You can't listen to your children all the time. My daughter tells me I don't wear clothing. I'm wearing clothing. My daughter, Janie, thinks I call her in the morning to check up on her. Yesterday she answered the phone and said, "Hello mother. This morning I got married, lost twenty pounds and became a lawyer."

LILLIAN. That's funny.

TASHA. Oh, you can always have a good time with Janie. But you know what's sad? Not sad like a child is ill or something. But a little sad to me. My daughter never thinks I call because I miss her. The girls at dancing school tell me their problems, they tell me about their parents, their boyfriends, what they ate yesterday, what they're going to eat tomorrow. But they're not my children. Sure, I'd like Janie to be married, and if she were a lawyer that'd be nice too, and believe me, if I could take her by the hand and do it for her I would, I'm that sort of mother. I remember when Janie was in high school and she'd slam the door to her room and say, "Mother, what do you want from me?" Lillian, what do I want from her? I just want to know that she's well. And to give her a little push too. But just a little one.

LILLIAN. (*Reassuring.*) Sooner or later you can have everything pressed.

TASHA. It's "everything presses itself out". I'll tell you. Life isn't like those Ivory Snow commercials with the mother and daughter comparing hands. Maybe your life is like that but at seven fifteen in the morning, my Janie and I don't get up to play golf together.

LILLIAN. Harriet and I don't get up to play golf either. (*Pause.*) Do those string beans really fill you up?

TASHA. You're an intelligent woman, Lillian, how could a bag of string beans really fill you up?

LILLIAN. Do you ever go to Rumpelmeyers across the street?

TASHA. I take my grandaughter when she's in the city.

LILLIAN. Rumpelmeyers always sold the nicest stuffed animals. I never liked the Steiff toys at F.A.O. Schwartz.

TASHA. They're made in Germany.

LILLIAN. How many grandchildren do you have?

TASHA. Just one. But I'm looking forward. I'll tell you what's nice about grandchildren. You don't have to worry about them everyday and they don't hoc you a chinic. That means they don't bang on your tea kettle.

LILLIAN. Would you join me at Rumpelmeyers for a sundae. I have twenty minutes before I have to go to a meeting. I'm sure you can get an iced coffee and some fruit.

TASHA. Why should I have fruit when they have such nice ice cream? I don't care what restaurant you go to the fresh fruit cup is never fresh.

LILLIAN. I haven't gone for a sundae in the afternoon since I was at Vassar. This is a big day for me. A frankfurter in the park, a sundae at Rumpelmeyers. I'm having a wonderful time.

TASHA. The girls at dancing school always say you can have a good time with Tasha.

LILLIAN. Do you like James Garner?

TASHA. Who?

LILLIAN. Do you ever watch the Rockford Files?

TASHA. I put the television on sometimes when I'm waiting for Simon to come home after my classes, but I don't really watch it. Just educational broadcasting and the Barbara Walter's Special. Did you see her with Richard Nixon the other week? That man did all right for himself.

LILLIAN. I beg your pardon.

TASHA. Both his daughters married well, he has a nice house, he travels, and what was he before, a Quacker.

LILLIAN. Excuse me.

TASHA. A Quaker. Listen I know you people don't like to get very intimate, but since our daughters are such good friends, I want to tell you I always admired you. You were always on time to all the parent-teacher meetings. Not that you and I both aren't smarter than all those teachers combined. But the other mothers would always come in late with the Louis Vuitton bags, and the manicures, but you, the only one who had something else important to do, you were always on time.

LILLIAN. Thank you.

TASHA. What are you thanking me for? You worked very hard. We both worked very hard. That's why we put out such nice products. (*They walk off arm in arm chatting. Tasha, as she exits:*) Do you remember that girl, Cynthia Peterson — well. . . .

END SCENE

TELEPHONE MACHINE #4

TAJLEI KAPLAN SINGLEBERRY. (*Ring. Beep.*) Miss Bloomberg, this is Tajlei Kaplan Singleberry at Sesame Street. Could you come in and see us next week. 288-7808, extension 22. Thank you.

HARRIET. (*Beep.*) Janie, it's Harriet. Would you do me an enormous favor? Would you and Marty come to dinner tomorrow night? Paul Stuart will be there. Don't ask. (*She begins to sing.*) "I love him. I love him. I love him. And where he goes I'll follow, I'll follow, I'll follow. . . ."*

END SCENE

*See Special Note on copyright page.

ACT TWO

Scene Two

Harriet's apartment. Janie, Marty & Harriet are having drinks.

HARRIET. My mother identifies with Jean Harris.

JANIE. I think Jean's mistake was stopping with Dr. Tarnover. On her way to Scarsdale she should have taken care of all of them. Dr. Atkins, Dr. Pritikin, the nut in Beverly Hills who says it's good to live on papaya.

MARTY. Monkey, Jean Harris should stay in jail for life. (*Marty's beeper goes off.*) I hear you Mrs. Rosen. I hear you. I was up all night with her. She thinks the dialysis machine is connected to my telephone. Do you have a private one I could use?

HARRIET. In the kitchen. (*Marty exits into kitchen. He looks back at Janie.*) He's sweet.

JANIE. He's very sweet. Sometimes I look at Marty and think he's such a nice young man, I must be a nice young girl.

HARRIET. You are.

JANIE. I never meant to become one. Last week, when we were driving up from yet another Sterling Tavern opening on the Island, I had my head in his lap and he stroked my hair and called me "Monkey". And at first I thought, Janie Jill Blumberg, you've been accepted, not even on the waiting list. So he calls you Monkey. You'd prefer what? Angel? Sweetheart?

HARRIET. Beauty?

JANIE. And I thought it's settled, fine, thank God. And I bet I can convince him that Schlomo is not a name for an American child. We were driving along the L.I.E. I was fantasizing if we'd make the Sunday Times wedding announcements, "Daughter of Pioneer in Interpretive Dance marries Pop-Over Boy. And it was just as we were approaching Syosset that I thought I can't breathe in this car and I promised myself that in a month from now I would not be travelling home from the Island in this car with Marty. And as soon as I thought this and honestly almost pushed open the car door, I found myself kissing his hand and saying, "Marty, I love you". I don't know.

HARRIET. I don't know either. Maybe Lillian is right. Life is much easier without relationships.

JANIE. Hattie, do you think I should live with Marty?

HARRIET. Well, if you live with him, you won't have to wonder who'll hold you at night, what will happen if you don't pay your taxes, or even if you want children who you could possibly get to be the father. You won't read articles in magazines about single women and have to think of the fifty different reasons why you're different than that. You won't begin to notice younger men on the street or think I'm not really hurting a married man's wife if I have an affair with him because if it's not me, it'll be somebody else. But Janie, how could you sleep next to a man as nice as Marty and lie to him and say I love you.

JANIE. I do love him. Maybe I'm just frightened.

HARRIET. I thought we had a pact. There's nothing wrong with being alone. We can wait til it's right. (*Marty enters.*) How's Mrs. Rosen?

MARTY. She died. Just kidneying. Actually, she's not happy with her donor so I'm driving her home to Rye.

HARRIET. Oh, I'm going up to Rye next week for a planning conference. My friend, Joe Stine, is driving me up there. (*Doorbell Rings.*) Maybe we can take Mrs. Rosen with us.

MARTY. Actually, I can't stay for dinner. The hospital wants me back in a half hour. (*To Janie.*) Who's Joe Stine?

JANIE. Some friend of Harriet's. I've never met him. (*Harriet has answered the door. Paul enters. His shoulder is stiff to his ear.*)

PAUL. I think I got whiplash on the cab ride down here.

HARRIET. I'm sorry. Are you all right?

PAUL. There's no way to get around safely in this city. God damn taxi driver went over a pot hole.

JANIE. Do you want Marty to have a look at your neck?

PAUL. It's not my neck. It's my left arm. Oh, my God. Maybe I'm having a heart attack.

MARTY. Really, I don't mind having a look at it.

JANIE. Marty's a resident at Mount Sinai.

PAUL. (*To Marty.*) Nice to meet you. (*Shakes his head.*)

MARTY. And this is Janie Blumberg.

PAUL. The only other possibility is my doctor says I've been taking too many amateur massages.

HARRIET. Paul, how about a drink?

PAUL. I better not with this neck thing.

39

MARTY. I can recommend a Chiropractor.

JANIE. I thought Chiropractors were quacks. My mother says Chiropractors are quacks. She's a dancer.

PAUL. Your mother's a dancer? What company is she with?

JANIE. She's an independent.

HARRIET. Sweet gherkins? Paul, remember the T.V. commercial we saw, well, Marty's father's the one who was giving away the shrimp.

PAUL. Oh, I loved it. I loved it. Is that kid's name really Schlomo?

MARTY. Yes. The UJA is really pissed at my father for making Schlomo eat shrimp on television.

PAUL. I love it. I love it.

HARRIET. More brie, Marty? (*To Paul.*) How are you feeling?

PAUL. I don't know, Honey. I have this sensation in my foot. Maybe this is a neurological thing.

JANIE. Well, maybe.

MARTY. Doesn't seem to be.

PAUL. What's your speciality?

MARTY. Kidneys.

PAUL. The kid's name is really Schlomo? I love it.

JANIE. You're in marketing, aren't you?

PAUL. Yes, but it's too boring to talk about.

HARRIET. I don't think it's boring. (*To Marty.*) Have some gherkins? (*Pause.*)

PAUL. Anyone seen anything good recently?

MARTY. God, I haven't been to a film in ages. If I get any time I try to read.

JANIE. Did you read the article in the Times about artificial insemination? I can imagine myself at 36, driving cross country to inseminate myself with a turkey baster.

PAUL. Turkey baster?

JANIE. Uh-huh. I'm going to give birth to a little oven stuffer roaster. (*Janie, Marty, and Harriet crack-up.*)

PAUL. (*Getting up.*) Well, I have to be going.

JANIE. Aren't you going to stay for dinner? There's chicken merango.

MARTY. Really, I wouldn't rush off because of the whiplash.

PAUL. Nice meeting both of you. Cathy . . er, Beauty, I'm just a little tired. (*He kisses Harriet on the cheek, picks up his coat and starts to leave.*)

HARRIET. Paul, I don't think we should see each other anymore. (*Paul stops. Janie & Marty slowly turn to Paul.*)

PAUL. Excuse me.

HARRIET. I want to stop.

PAUL. (*Moves down to Harriet and whispers.*) We've been through this before.

MARTY. Harriet, do you want Janie and I to get dessert?

HARRIET. No.

PAUL. C'mon Harriet. I've got this neck thing. Your friends are here. We'll talk about it tomorrow. We'll have breakfast. What's the matter, Beauty, do you have your period?

MARTY. (*Standing with Janie.*) See you later.

HARRIET. Don't go. (*They sit.*) Paul's leaving to catch up on his laundry.

PAUL. You knew what the parameters were here. You're a very appealing woman, Harriet. It's nice meeting both of you. Thanks for helping me with this neck thing. Beauty, calm down. You're a good kid. (*He snaps his fingers as if to say "see you later" and exits.*)

MARTY. He's crazy. He didn't have whiplash. Harriet, he's the least gracious man I ever met. In fact, he's a real douche.

JANIE. Hattie, I'm sorry.

HARRIET. What are you sorry for? (*She exits L.*)

JANIE. I shouldn't have told him about artificial insemination.

HARRIET. (*Entering.*) I'm going for a walk.

JANIE. When are you coming back?

HARRIET. Janie, you sound like Tasha. I don't know when I'm coming back. (*Harriet exits out the front door.*)

JANIE. Well, this was a real nice clambake. I'm mighty glad I came.

MARTY. Why is she seeing that guy?.

JANIE. The sadist vice-president at Colgate Palmolive? I don't know.

MARTY. Monkey.

JANIE. What?

MARTY. My father wants to know if we're coming to dinner tomorrow. It's my brother's anniversary. The whole family will be there.

JANIE. I can't. I got a call from Sesame Street. They want to interview me. I have to stay home and put together some sketches for the giant bird.

MARTY. So you'll do it next week. What?

JANIE. Nothing.

MARTY. What nothing, Monkey?

JANIE. Nothing. Nothing.

MARTY. You want to interview at Sesame Street, fine. They do nice work. But don't let it take over your life. And don't let it take over our life. That's a real trap.

JANIE. Marty, I haven't even interviewed there yet. (*He rubs her back intermittently, tapping as if he's checking her heart.*)

MARTY. You're a sweet woman. You don't want a life like that.

JANIE. Like what?

MARTY. Look, I have plenty of friends who marry women doctors because they think they'll have something in common. Monkey, they never see each other. Their children are brought up by strangers from the Caribbean.

JANIE. That's a nice way of putting it.

MARTY. I have nothing against your working. I just want to make sure we have a life.

JANIE. Marty, I like my work. I may have stumbled into something I actually care about. And right now I don't want to do it part-time and pretend that it's real when it would actually be a hobby. But I want a life too. Honey, my mother takes my father skating every Saturday. Simon and that dancer have struck up a partnership. I'm their daughter. I want that too.

MARTY. Janie, I made arrangements with the Sterling truck to move us to Brooklyn next Saturday.

JANIE. We're gonna move with a lot of shrimp and lobster tails?

MARTY. What are you trying to do, entertain me like you tried to entertain Paul Stuart?

JANIE. I was just trying . . .

MARTY. You know what, Monkey, you're a little disorganized, I'm a little bit of a nudge. So if I don't make the arrangements, what's going to happen? You'll live alone or maybe you'll meet someone who's even more of a nudge.

JANIE. Marty, if I'm one of the few real people you've met,

42

why do you call me, "Monkey"?

MARTY. Jesus, Janie, I'm just trying to move us foward. I gotta go. I'm on call this week. I'll see you on Saturday. (*Marty snaps his fingers as if he's imitating Paul. Marty exits. Janie walks around the sofa, slowly turns and gasps.*)

END SCENE

TELEPHONE MACHINE #5

VLADIMIR. (*Ring. Beep.*) Hello-hi. This is Vladimir. Hello-hi. Uh, I have tickets for Bruce Springsteen. I will return call. (*Hang up.*)
CYNTHIA PETERSON. (*Beep.*) Janie, it's Cynthia Peterson. I met a man on a plane to Houston. Keep your fingers crossed. (*Hang up.*)

END SCENE

ACT TWO

Scene Three

Four Seasons Restaurant. Harriet & Lillian seated at a table. They have finished eating their entrees. Harriet is distracted.

LILLIAN. Everything all right with you?
HARRIET. Fine. I guess. I made a presentation to my boss a week ago. He told me my ideas were too theoretical. Then the next day, at a meeting, my friend Joe Stine said my boss presented my ideas as his own and he got them through.
LILLIAN. Good for you.
HARRIET. Mother I work very hard. I don't want that man stealing my ideas.
LILLIAN. You think it would be better to be married and have your husband steal your ideas?
HARRIET. What?
LILLIAN. I was just cheering you up with a depressing alternative. Look at Jean Harris. That guy would have manipulated

her for the rest of her life. Do me a favor, baby. Go in tomorrow and tell your boss, whoever he is, Ron, Rick, Dick, I am sorry but you stole my idea and I hold you accountable. (*Pause.*) Do you want dessert? Have some chocolate velvet cake and I'll take a taste.

HARRIET. Mother, you haven't finished not eating your lunch. You haven't picked all the salad dressing off your salad or removed all the potatoes from your plate.

LILLIAN. Tom, we'll have the chocolate velvet cake.

HARRIET. I remember when you took me here as a little girl. I told everyone in my class we were going to the Four Seasons for lunch cause you told me it was very special. And I always loved coming here and I thought you were very beautiful in your subtle blue suits, calling all those grown men, Tom, Dave. I mean, they never really knew the other women in the room, but they knew my mommy. My mommy was important.

LILLIAN. She is. Harriet you can't blame everything on me. I wasn't home enough for you to blame everything on me.

HARRIET. Clever.

LILLIAN. I thought so. (*Waves to someone.*) Hi, Bill.

HARRIET. Are you proud of me?

LILLIAN. Of course I'm proud of you. Are you proud of me?

HARRIET. Yes. Very.

LILLIAN. I didn't cheat you too much.

HARRIET. No.

LILLIAN. Have children, Harriet. It's one of the few things in life that's worthwhile. (*She waves at another man.*) Hi, Kip.

HARRIET. Mother, when do you stop hoping that there will be some enormous change, some dam breaking and then you'll start living your life? You know what I'm tired of? I'm tired of the whole idea that everything takes work. Relationships take work, personal growth takes work, spiritual development, child rearing, creativity. Well, I would like to do something simply splendidly that took absolutely no real effort at all.

LILLIAN. Harriet, your thinking is all over the place today. What is it? Are you having an affair or something?

HARRIET. My boss's boss. The one you said should be further along. But it's nothing.

LILLIAN. 40% of the people at McKinsey are having affairs.

HARRIET. I know that.

LILLIAN. See how nice it is to have a daughter in your own field. If you want me to, I'd like to meet this guy.

HARRIET. It's over. He once had an interview with you. He said you have balls.

LILLIAN. Don't be offended baby. Your father said the same thing. (*She waves again.*) Hi, Ken. Where's our cake? I have a meeting at 2:30.

HARRIET. Mother. . . ?

LILLIAN. What is this, "Youth wants to know"? Honey, I'm an old lady. I don't know all the answers to these things.

HARRIET. I have just one more question. Just one.

LILLIAN. To get to the other side.

HARRIET. What?

LILLIAN. I was giving you the answer.

HARRIET. That's not funny.

LILLIAN. I'm not a funny woman. Ask me, baby, I've got to go. Where is that man? I can't sit around here like this.

HARRIET. Calm down.

LILLIAN. What's your question? Harriet, I'm in a hurry.

HARRIET. Mother, do you think it's possible to be married or living with a man, have a good relationship and children that you share equal responsibility for, and a career, and still read novels, play the piano, have women friends and swim twice a week?

LILLIAN. You mean what the women's magazines call, "Having it all"? Harriet, that's just your generation's fantasy.

HARRIET. Mother, you're being too harsh. Listen to me, what I want to know is if you do have all those things, my generation's fantasy, then what do you want?

LILLIAN. Needlepoint. You desperately want to needlepoint. (*Pause.*) Life is a negotiation, Harriet. You think the women who go back to work at 36 are going to have the same career as a woman who has been there since her twenties? You think someone who has a baby and leaves it after two weeks to go back to work is going to have the same relationship with that child as someone who has been there all along? It's impossible. And you show me the wonderful man with whom you're going to have it all. You tell me how he feels when you take as many business trips as he does. You tell me who has to leave the office when the kid bumps his head on a radiator or slips on a milk carton.

45

No, I don't think what you asked me is possible.

HARRIET. All right. When you were 29, what was possible for you?

LILLIAN. When I was your age, I realized I had to make some choices. I had a promising career, a child, and a husband; and believe me, if you have all three, and you're very conscientious, you still have to choose your priorities. So I gave some serious thought to what was important to me. And what was important to me was a career I could be proud of and successfully bringing up a child. So the first thing that had to go was pleasing my husband cause he was a grown-up and could take care of himself. Yes, baby, everything did take work; but it was worthwhile. I never dreamed I'd be this successful. And I have a perfectly lovely daughter. Baby, I have a full, rich life.

HARRIET. Mommy, what full, rich life? You watch Rockford File reruns every night.

LILLIAN. If a man more appealing then James Garner comes into my life, I'll make room for him too. O.K., Baby?

HARRIET. Well, I've made up my mind. I'm going to try to do it. Have it all.

LILLIAN. Good for you. For your sake, I hope you can. (*Pause.*) What's the matter, Harriet? Did I disillusion you?

HARRIET. No, I'm afraid I'm just like you.

LILLIAN. Don't be afraid. You're younger.

HARRIET. Mother, you're trying my patience.

LILLIAN. You sound just like me, dear.

HARRIET. If you were younger, I'd say something nasty.

LILLIAN. Whisper it late at night. It will give you guilt and anxiety. Your sweet old Mom who worked for years to support you.

HARRIET. Fuck off, mother.

LILLIAN. Don't tell that to your boss. Pay the bill, will you. Comb your hair, baby. I like it better off your face. Call me Sunday. Pretend it's Mother's Day. (*To waiter.*) This young lady will take the check please. I love you, Harriet. (*Lillian kisses her on the cheek.*)

HARRIET. I love you, too.

LILLIAN. Sometimes.

HARRIET. Sometimes.

LILLIAN. (*As she exits.*) Lovely lunch, Tom. Thank you. (*Harriet takes out her American Express Gold Card and lays it on the table.*)

END SCENE

TELEPHONE MACHINE #6

SIMON. (*Ring. Beep.*) Janie, it's Dad. Do you want to meet us at Oscar's for brunch? (*Hang up.*)

MARTY. Monkey, sweetheart, are you there? Pick it up. Pick it up. I have to do my father a big favor tomorrow in Central Park. You and I will have dinner in Brooklyn. (*Hang up.*)

END SCENE

ACT TWO

Scene Four

Central Park. We hear Sousa's, "Washington Post". * Marty enters to cheers. He picks up a mike. Camera flashes go off.

MARTY. (*Into microphone.*) This is Dr. Murray Schlimovitz standing in for my father, Captain Milty. I'm here at beautiful Central Park to inaugurate the first Annual Sterling Marathon. That's right. He's giving away Spring Water, he's giving away Seltzer, he's giving away Carob Bars. (*Janie enters* L.) And you know what my father always says. "You should only live and be well." (*Marty waves and the crowd cheers. He puts down the mike and moves to Janie.*) Janie?
JANIE. Hi, Dr. Murray Schlimovitz.
MARTY. I decided to open my practice in Brooklyn under my real name. What are you doing here?
JANIE. I was in the neighborhood. They accepted my sketches for the giant bird. Does Mount Sinai know you're here?

*See Special Note on copyright page.

47

MARTY. I'm here because it's my responsibility to my family. (*Pause.*) Oy, I'm such a schmucky nice doctor.

JANIE. You're not such a schmucky nice doctor. What's the matter?

MARTY. I don't understand you. I call you all last night to coordinate the time for the moving truck to arrive at your house today, you don't return my calls, and then you arrive here today ready to crack jokes. Janie, what are you, a home entertainment unit? Honey, go home. The moving truck will be at your house in an hour.

JANIE. Marty, do you ever get the feeling that everything is changing and you don't know when you decided to make the change?

MARTY. Nothing's changing. I'm offering you love, I'm offering you affection, I'm offering you attention. All you have to do is put your crates that you never unpacked on that truck and get on the Belt Parkway. You just move forward.

JANIE. I can't just move forward.

MARTY. You know what I think? I think you're frightened to try. You think it's a compromise. You think you're not grown-up yet. That's bullshit. Maybe you think I'm not special enough.

JANIE. I think you're very special. But I want us to decide to move when we decide together. Marty, you took an apartment and you didn't even tell me about it first. None of it had anything to do with me. I don't want to sneak around you and pretend that I'm never angry. I don't want to be afraid of you. I guess to a man I love I want to feel not just that I can talk, but that you'll listen.

MARTY. Do you think I don't listen to you?

JANIE. You have all the answers before I ask the questions.

MARTY. You picked a hell of a time to bring this up. You want to give the answers, fine. You make the decision right now. Either you move in with me tonight or we stop and I'll make alternate arrangements.

JANIE. Marty, by you everything is much more simple than it has to be. You want a wife, you get a wife. You drop out of Harvard twice, they always take you back. You're just like me. We're too fucking sweet. I'm so sweet, I never say what I want, and you're so sweet, you always get what you want.

MARTY. Not necessarily. Why do you think I'm thirty-two and not married? All I want is a home, a family, something my father had so easily and I can't seem to get started on. Why? I'm a nice Jewish doctor. Women want to marry their daughters off to me all the time. Sure, I want to know where I'll live, who'll take the children to the nursery, but I wanted something special too. Just a little. Maybe not as special as you turned out to be, but just a little. Janie, I do not want to marry anyone like my sister-in-law.

JANIE. I never liked her. Honey, I wish we could throw a wedding at the Plaza. And your father could be Toastmaster General, and Harriet would select my pattern, and my mother would dance, and baby Schlomo could carry the ring in one of my father's gold seal envelopes.

MARTY. (*Cuts her off suddenly, quite angry.*) Goddamit, Janie, make a decision! You want to have children with a turkey baster, that's fine. You want to write sketches for a giant bird at two o'clock in the morning, that's fine too, you wanna come home to Cynthia Peterson's phone calls, great. You want to find out what it's like to take care of yourself, good luck to you. But it isn't right for me. And I'll tell you something, Janie, it isn't right for you either.

JANIE. (*Softly.*) Marty, you're not right for me. I can't move in with you now. If I did that, I'd always be a monkey, a sweet little girl.

MARTY. (*After a pause.*) I have to get back with the starting pistol. (*He starts to go. Janie stops him.*)

JANIE. Honey, it's complicated.

MARTY. No. It's simple. You don't love me enough. (*Marty exits.*)

JANIE. Marty. . . . (*After a pause, we hear Marty on a microphone, offstage.*)

MARTY. This is Dr. Murray Schlimovitz. At the First Annual Sterling Marathon. Runners ready. On your marks. Get set. Go. (*Janie is left alone on stage as lights fade.*)

END SCENE

TELEPHONE MACHINE #7

HARRIET. (*Ring. Beep.*) Janie, I have good news. No, great news. Can you and Marty come over to dinner Sunday at 6:00? There's Chicken Merango. Bye. (*Hang up.*)
HARRIET. (*Beep.*) Harriet, again. Where are you? If you guys don't show up tomorrow, I'll hock your china. I miss you . . (*Hang up.*)
OPERATOR. (*Dial Tone.*) Please hang up. There seems to be a receiver off the hook.

END SCENE

ACT TWO

Scene Five

Harriet's apartment. Lillian and Harriet, with a drink.

HARRIET. I thought you'd tell me I was insane.
LILLIAN. You're not insane. Impetuous, but not insane. Does Janie like Joe?
HARRIET. Janie's never even met Joe.
LILLIAN. You should talk to her about him. It's important to discuss your life choices with your friends.
HARRIET. Mother, you're so full of homespun advice today.
LILLIAN. I got my hair done yesterday. I read a lot of those women's magazines. You and Joe will have to come over next week for some jello. (*Doorbell rings. Harriet answers it. Janie is there with a bouquet of flowers.*)
JANIE. (*Offstage.*) Harriet, it's me, Janie.
HARRIET. (*Opening door.*) Hi.
JANIE. These are for you. I was afraid you'd say they're too old, they're too new, they're gold.
HARRIET. No, they're perfect. (*Harriet points Janie to her mother.*)
JANIE. How are you Mrs. Cornwall?
LILLIAN. Janie, I'll know you the rest of my life and you'll still call me, Mrs. Cornwall. Makes me feel good, baby. The kids in

50

my office call me Lillian and pretend we're colleagues. We're not colleagues. I'm a person of moral and intellectual superiority.

HARRIET. (*From off, kitchen.*) My mother deals from strength. (*She enters with drink for Janie.*)

JANIE. Speaking of strength, guess who called me? Paul Stuart. He said to tell you he really likes you very much and he doesn't understand why you won't return his calls. I'm *awfully* glad he has my number.

LILLIAN. Is this your boss's boss? The one who was so impressed with my potency.

HARRIET. Well, he's my boss now. I was promoted.

HARRIET and JANIE. Yeah!!!! (*Janie and Harriet hug.*)

JANIE. I knew there was good news here. I got the chicken merango message and I said something good was happening. I've been trying to call you but you weren't home and then I was busy sending the letter, "B", to the Bahamas. "Sesame Street" hired me part time!

HARRIET and JANIE. Yeah!!!! (*Janie and Harriet hug again.*)

LILLIAN. Perhaps, I should feel threatened. I'm surrounded by a generation of achieving younger women.

HARRIET. I don't think Janie's threatening to anyone. That's her gift.

LILLIAN. Well, she's impressive. (*Pause.*) Where's your nice young man? Harriet said she invited him to dinner tonight. I was looking forward to meeting him.

JANIE. Uh, Marty's busy tonight. There's a testimonial dinner for his father at Szechuan Taste. One day they'll find out which Rabbi he's paying off and close down those places.

LILLIAN. Harriet, maybe Marty's father should cater your wedding? It'll be a first for the Plaza. And we could keep it in the family.

JANIE. (*Not hearing what she said.*) Excuse me?

HARRIET. Janie, do you remember at my Whiplash Party two weeks ago, I told you I was driving up to a planning conference with Joe? He's the headhunter who got me my job at Colgate. He was a year ahead of me at Harvard. I've been spending a lot of time with him recently. And yesterday, he asked me to marry him.

JANIE. What?

HARRIET. (*Harriet stands up and announces with pride.*) I'm going to marry Joe Stine. (*Pause.*)

LILLIAN. He'll be all right for a first husband. I'm just kidding. You know I'm thrilled, baby.

JANIE. Congratulations!

HARRIET. I would have told you earlier, but I didn't even know it was happening. And my time with Joe has been so intense. I wasn't able to call you.

JANIE. That's wonderful!

LILLIAN. Janie, you and I will have to plan the shower together. Well, I'm off to the Ming Dynasty.

HARRIET. What?

LILLIAN. I'm taking an Art History class. Not for credit. Your mother is broadening herself. I'll leave you girls to your dinner. Harriet, for the sake of your marriage, move beyond Chicken Merango. Bye bye girls. (*Lillian exits.*)

JANIE. She's in a good mood.

HARRIET. She's been reading Redbook. So, what do you think?

JANIE. It's wonderful. Mazel Tov.

HARRIET. (*Exiting to kitchen.*) I didn't mean to surprise you like this. I wanted to have you and Marty to dinner. Are things O.K. with Marty?

JANIE. Yeah, Fine.

HARRIET. You O.K.?

JANIE. Harriet, have you thought about living with Joe first? Better yet, maybe you should have dinner with Joe first?

HARRIET. I want to marry him. Janie, he's the only person who's even cared about me in a long time. He listens to me. (*Harriet enters with flowers in a vase.*) Tasha's right. You and I deserve a little nachos.

JANIE. Naches.

HARRIET. Joe makes me feel like I have a family. I never had a family. I had you and Lillian but I never felt I could have what other women just assumed they would get.

JANIE. I want to know one thing. I want to know why when I asked you about my living with Marty, you told me you didn't respect women who didn't learn to live alone and pay their own rent? And then, the first chance you have to change your life, you grasp it.

52

HARRIET. What? Marrying Joe is just a chance that just came along.

JANIE. I see. You've been waiting for some man to come along and change your life. And all the things you told me about learning to live alone and women and friendship, that was so much social nonsense. I feel like an idiot! I made choices based on an idea that doesn't exist anymore.

HARRIET. What choices?

JANIE. Never mind.

HARRIET. Janie, when I told you that, I didn't know what it would be like when Paul Stuart would leave at 10:00 and go home to Cathy and I would have to pretend I wasn't hurt. I didn't know what it would be like to have lunch with Lillian and think I'm on my way to watching Rockford File reruns. Of course you should learn to live alone and pay your own rent, but I didn't realize what it would feel like for me when I became too good at it. Janie, I know how to come home, put on the news, have a glass of wine, read a book, call you. What I don't know is what to do when there's someone who loves me in the house.

JANIE. I could throw this table at you.

HARRIET. Why? Janie, we're too good friends for you to be jealous.

JANIE. I'm not jealous.

HARRIET. Don't blame me for your doubts about Marty.

JANIE. Harriet, I don't blame you for anything. I'm sorry. Right now I just don't like you very much.

HARRIET. Why? Because I'm leaving you? Because I'm getting married?

JANIE. Because our friendship didn't mean very much to you. You buy me the sugar, the bread and the salt and you stand there and tell me you never had a family. Harriet, you never really listened to me and you never really told me about yourself. And that's sad.

HARRIET. Janie, I love you. But you want us to stay girls together. I'm not a girl anymore. I'm almost thirty and I'm alone.

JANIE. You lied to me.

HARRIET. I never lied to you. I lied to myself. It doesn't take any strength to be alone, Janie. It's much harder to be with someone also. I want to have children and get on with my life.

JANIE. What do you do? Fall in with every current the tide pulls in? Women should live alone and find out what they can do, put off marriage, establish a vertical career track, so you do that for a while. Then you almost turn thirty and Time Magazine announces "Guess what girls, it's time to have it all". Jaclyn Smith is married and pregnant and playing Jacqueline Kennedy. Every other person who was analyzing stocks last year is analyzing layettes this year. So you do that. What are you doing, Harriet? Who the hell are you? Can't you conceive of some plan, some time management scheme that you made up for yourself? Can't you take a chance? *(Exit to kitchen w/ glasses)*

HARRIET. I am taking a chance. I hardly know this man.

JANIE. You don't have to force yourself into a situation—a marriage because it's time.

HARRIET. You're just frightened of being with someone, Janie. You're just frightened of making a choice and taking responsibility for it.

JANIE. That sounds romantic.

HARRIET. That's life.

JANIE. Harriet, you're getting married to someone you've been dating for two weeks. I am much more scared of being alone than you are. But I'm not going to turn someone into the answer for me.

HARRIET. Then you'll be alone.

JANIE. Then I'll be alone. (*Pause.*) I better go. I have to get up early with the letter "B". If they like this, they'll hire me full time. In charge of consonants.

HARRIET. Give my love to Marty.

JANIE. I can't. I told him I won't move with him to Brooklyn.

HARRIET. So you'll get an apartment in Manhattan.

JANIE. (*She cries.*) We broke up. I decided not to see him anymore.

HARRIET. Won't you miss him?

JANIE. I missed him today when I saw someone who looks sweet like him walking down the street and I'll miss him late tonight.

HARRIET. Maybe you should call him.

JANIE. No.

HARRIET. Life is a negotiation.

JANIE. I don't believe I have to believe that.

HARRIET. Janie, it's too painful not to grow up.

JANIE. That's not how I want to grow up. (*Janie kisses Harriet and starts to go.*) (walk over to table)

HARRIET. You don't have to separate from me. I'm not leaving you.

JANIE. (*Picking up trash.*) Want me to throw this out for you?

HARRIET. Sure.

JANIE. Do you really think anyone has ever met someone throwing out the garbage? (*They both shake their head no. Janie exits.*)

END SCENE

ACT TWO

Scene Six

Janie's apartment. Janie is alone, sitting in front of her crates, wrapped in her blanket, holding a swizzle stick and crying. We hear a romantic version of the song "Isn't It Romantic."* The doorbell rings. No answer. Doorbell rings again.

SIMON. (*From offstage.*) Janie, Janie.

JANIE. (*Softly.*) What? (*Doorbell rings.*)

SIMON. Janie. Janie. It's Dad. Can we come in?

JANIE. Just a second.

TASHA. (*Offstage.*) Janie, the super said he doesn't have the key.

JANIE. (*Crossing to door.*) I changed the lock.

TASHA. (*Offstage.*) What?!

JANIE. Mother, you can't come in until you repeat after me. My daughter is a grown woman.

TASHA. (*Offstage.*) Simon, she's crazy.

JANIE. My daughter is a grown woman.

TASHA. (*Offstage.*) My daughter is a grown woman.

*See Special Note on copyright page.

JANIE. This is her apartment.

TASHA. (*Offstage.*) Of course, it's your apartment.

SIMON. (*Offstage.*) For Christ's sake, just tell her. . . .

TASHA. (*Offstage.*) This is her apartment.

JANIE. I am to call before I arrive here.

TASHA. (*Offstage.*) I always call. I get the machine.

SIMON. (*Offstage.*) Janie, we can leave this with the doorman.

JANIE. There isn't any doorman here.

TASHA. (*Offstage.*) Simon, maybe she wants to be alone.

JANIE. (*Opens the door.*) It's all right, mother. The six truck drivers just left out the back window. (*Tasha & Simon enter. He carries a box.*)

SIMON. Sorry to bother you. We tried calling, but you don't return our calls.

JANIE. I've been busy, Daddy. I'm going on location with the letter, "C" to Canada. They seem to like me.

TASHA. Of course they like you. You're my daughter.

JANIE. I don't think they *know you* mother.

TASHA. Simon, give her the package and let's go. (*Simon puts down the box.*) Your father said Janie will look like a model in this.

SIMON. You don't have to keep it unless you like it. (*Janie opens the box. It contains a mink coat.*) Do you like it?

TASHA. Give your father a little pleasure. Try it on. (*Tasha helps Janie with it, it is very small. She hunches to pull it around her.*)

SIMON. I think it's very nice to your face. The girls are wearing the sleeves short now.

TASHA. I see girls your age wearing theirs to walk the baby carriage.

SIMON. Don't say you like it, if you don't like it.

JANIE. I like it. I like it. If I was 36 and married to a doctor and a size three, this would be perfect for me.

TASHA. So why aren't you?

JANIE. Do you really want to know why I don't call you? You expect me to dial the phone and say, "Hello mother, hello father, here I am in my mink coat. I just came home from wearing it to walk the carriage. Everything is settled. Eveything has worked out wonderfully. Here are your naches. Congratulations. I appreciate you."

TASHA. Why do you speak so much Yiddish? We never spoke

so much Yiddish around the house.

JANIE. Look, I'm sorry. Things didn't work out as you planned. There's nothing wrong with that life, it just isn't mine right now.

SIMON. What are you getting so emotional about? Sit. Relax. Look at me. I never get so emotional. Janie, all we did was give you a coat. You'll wear it when its cold. And if you like, you'll wear it when it's hot like the old ladies in Miami. That's all. No big deal. Are you taking drugs? Your eyes are glossy. Dear, look at her eyes.

TASHA. I don't want to look at her eyes. You know, Janie, I'll never forget as a child when I sent you to Helena Rubenstein Charm School. And you always came late with the hair in the eyes and the hem hanging down. And Mrs. Rubenstein told me you were an ungrateful child.

JANIE. Mrs. Rubenstein never told you I was an ungrateful child.

TASHA. Simon, what did she tell us?

JANIE. The receptionist at Helena Rubenstein told you I was an ungrateful child. Mother, what do you want from me? You give me a mink coat and I know you think any other daughter would appreciate this. Helena Rubenstein knows any other daughter would appreciate this. Georgette Klinger's daughter would appreciate this. I'm a selfish, spoiled person. Something is the matter with me.

TASHA. (*Getting up.*) Something is the matter with you. Simon, I have to go dance. I have to work her out of my system.

SIMON. Dear, relax.

JANIE. I don't see how I can help you understand what I'm doing. Neither of you ever lived alone, you never thought maybe I won't have children and what will I do with my life if I don't.

TASHA. All right, you're the smart one. I'm the stupid one. I haven't taught you anything.

JANIE. (*Furious.*) Mother, think about it. Did you teach me to marry a nice Jewish doctor and make chicken for him? You order up breakfast from a Greek coffee shop every morning. Did you teach me to go to Law School and wear grey suits at a job that I sort of like everyday from 9–8? You run out of here in leg warmers and tank tops to dancing school. Did you teach me to compromise and lie to the man I live with and say I love you

57

when I wasn't sure? You live with your partner, you walk Dad to work every morning.

TASHA. Now I understand. Everything is my fault. I should have been like the other mothers, 40 chickens in the freezer and played Mah-jongg all afternoon. Janie, I couldn't live like that, God forbid. You think your father would have been happy with one of those women with the blond hair and the diamonds? And I'll tell you something else, you and Ben wouldn't have come out as well as you did. I believe a person should have a little originality — a little, you know. Otherwise you just grow old like everybody else. Let's go Simon. Honey, you don't have to call us. You don't even have to let us know how you are. You do what you want. (*Tasha starts to go.*)

JANIE. Wait a minute.

TASHA. I'm a modern woman too, you know. I have my dancing, I have your father, and my beautiful grandchild, and Ben. I don't need you to fill up my life. I'm an independent woman — a person in my own right. Am I right, Simon?

SIMON. Janie, as for me, what I want is some Sunday before I come over here with a coffee table or a mink coat, you'd call me and say, "Dad, let's get together, I'd like to see you".

TASHA. She doesn't want to see us.

JANIE. (*Pause, looking at her parents.*) I do want to see you. And you don't have to call every morning to sing, "Sunrise — Sunset", and you don't have to bring a mink coat or a coffee table, or even a Russian taxi cab driver for me to marry.

SIMON. What happened to him? He was a nice boy.

JANIE. All you have to do is trust me a little bit. I believe a person should have a little originality, a little you know, otherwise you just grow old like everybody else. And you know Janie, I like life-life-life. Mother, sit, relax, let me figure it out.

TASHA. But, Honey, if I sit, who's going to dance?

JANIE. Everything presses itself out.

TASHA. Unfortunately, Janie, the clock has a funny habit of keeping on ticking. I want to know who's going to take care of you when we're not around anymore.

JANIE. I guess I will. (*Janie takes her mother's hand.*) Mother, don't worry. I'm Tasha's daughter. I know, "I am".

TASHA. That's right. I am. (*Tasha is crying slightly. Janie touches Tasha's cheek, then they embrace.*)

SIMON. And Janie, from a man's point of view, the next time someone wants you to make him chicken, you tell him I was at your sister-in-law Christ's house the other day, and she ordered up lamb chops from the Madison Delicatessen. How hard is it to cook lamb chops? You just stick them in the broiler. If Christ can order up lamb chops, and she's a girl from Nebraska, you don't have to make anybody chicken. Believe me, you were born to order up.

JANIE. Sounds like manifest destiny.

SIMON. In fact, I have the number. We could have a family dinner right now.

TASHA. No, Simon, let's go home.

SIMON. (*Kisses Janie.*) Goodbye, Janie.

JANIE. Goodbye, Daddy.

TASHA. Goodbye honey.

JANIE. Mother, one more thing. Take back your mink. (*Janie takes it off and puts it over Tasha's shoulders.*)

TASHA. Fits me perfectly.

JANIE. Fits you perfectly.

TASHA. Where's my partner? (*Tasha sweeps up to Simon and arm-in-arm, they exit. Janie is alone for a moment, in silence. She takes a deep breath. She picks up her blanket and folds it neatly, picks up the mink box and sets them on a crate. It's time to finally unpack. She lifts all of the above and starts to exit into the bedroom as the telephone rings. Janie enters.*)

CYNTHIA PETERSON. (*On phone machine.*) Janie, it's Cynthia Peterson. It's my 34th Birthday. I'm alone. Nothing happened with Mr. Houston. I should have married Mark Silverstein in college. Janie, by the time I'm thirty five, this is what I want.

JANIE. (*Flaps her foot.*) Flap.

CYNTHIA PETERSON. I want 100,000 dollars a year, a husband, a baby. Janie, are you there? I hear breathing.

JANIE. (*Takes another step.*) Flap heel.

CYNTHIA PETERSON. I think someone's there. Whoever you are, there's nothing there worth taking.

JANIE. (*Moves and taps.*) Flap, flap, flap, touch. Flap, flap, flap, touch.

CYNTHIA PETERSON. Janie, I met a man at the deli last night. He asked me if I wanted to have a beer in his apartment at one o'clock in the morning. Do you think I should have gone?

59

(*Janie starts to tap with some assurance as the tape continues.*) There was an article in the New York Post that there are 1000 men for every 1123 New York hubby hunters. (*Music comes in [Isn't it Romantic]* as Janie crosses up and picks up hat and umbrella.*) And there was this picture of an eligible man. He's an actor and he likes painting. I like painting. Should I call him? (*The music gets louder, Janie dances as Cynthia fades. A spot picks up Janie dancing beautifully, alone.*) I could take him to the Guggenheim with my membership. How many of these 1123 women are going to call him? How many have memberships to the Guggenheim? I don't know if I want to marry an actor. Maybe I should wait for tomorrow's eligible bachelor. (*Spot fades on Janie, turning with the hat and umbrella.*)

END OF PLAY

*See Special Note on copyright page.

PROPERTY LIST

Act 1, Scene 1:
Can of Tab

Act 1, Scene 2:
Attache case
Boxes and crates (onstage)
Walkman tape recorder and earphones
Bag with coffee and sandwich
Envelope
Dollar bills

Act 1, Scene 3:
Gift box
Three noisemakers
Phone (onstage)

Act 1, Scene 5:
Binaca
Rolling bar with drinking glasses

Act 1, Scene 6:
Boxes and crates (onstage)
Typewriter (onstage)
Package
Bar
Box
Hallah bread
Kosher salt
Sugar
Matches
Candles

Act 1, Scene 7:
T.V.'s (2 — onstage)
Coffee table
Bag of groceries
Chicken in butcher paper

Act 2, Scene 1:
Towel
Hot dog
Bag of string beans

Act 2, Scene 2:
Drinking glasses

Act 2, Scene 3:
American Express gold card

Act 2, Scene 4:
Microphone (onstage)

Act 2, Scene 5:
Drinking glasses
Bouquet of flowers
Vase

Act 2, Scene 6:
Swizzle stick (onstage)
Blanket (onstage)
Hat (onstage)
Umbrella (onstage)
Mink coat

SOUND CUES

Prologue:
Phone ring
Answering machine beep
Dial tone
Phone hang up

Act 1, Scene 2:
Doorbell
Aerobic dance music

Act 1, Scene 3:
Phone buzz
Intercom buzz

Act 1, Scene 6:
Doorbell

Act 1, Scene 7:
Doorbell
Phone ring

Act 2, Scene 2:
Doorbell

Act 2, Scene 4:
Sousa's "Washington Post March"
Crowd cheers

Act 2, Scene 6:
Phone ring
Doorbell
Song "Isn't It Romantic?"

Telephone Machine 2:
Phone ring
Answering machine beep
Dial tone
Phone hang up

Telephone Machine 3:
Answering machine beep
Phone hang up

Telephone Machines 4,5,6,7:
Phone ring
Answering machine beep
Phone hang up

TODAY'S HOTTEST NEW PLAYS

❏ **MOLLY SWEENEY by Brian Friel, Tony Award-Winning Author of** *Dancing at Lughnasa.* Told in the form of monologues by three related characters, *Molly Sweeney* is mellifluous, Irish storytelling at its dramatic best. Blind since birth, Molly recounts the effects of an eye operation that was intended to restore her sight but which has unexpected and tragic consequences. *"Brian Friel has been recognized as Ireland's greatest living playwright. Molly Sweeney confirms that Mr. Friel still writes like a dream. Rich with rapturous poetry and the music of rising and falling emotions...Rarely has Mr. Friel written with such intoxicating specificity about scents, colors and contours." - New York Times.* [2M, 1W]

❏ **SWINGING ON A STAR (The Johnny Burke Musical) by Michael Leeds. 1996 Tony Award Nominee for Best Musical.** The fabulous songs of Johnny Burke are perfectly represented here in a series of scenes jumping from a 1920s Chicago speakeasy to a World War II USO Show and on through the romantic high jinks of the Bob Hope/Bing Crosby "Road Movies." Musical numbers include such favorites as "Pennies from Heaven," "Misty," "Ain't It a Shame About Mame," "Like Someone in Love," and, of course, the Academy Award winning title song, "Swinging on a Star." *"A WINNER. YOU'LL HAVE A BALL!" - New York Post. "A dazzling, toe-tapping, finger-snapping delight!" - ABC Radio Network. "Johnny Burke wrote his songs with moonbeams!" - New York Times.* [3M, 4W]

❏ **THE MONOGAMIST by Christopher Kyle.** Infidelity and mid-life anxiety force a forty-something poet to reevaluate his 60s values in a late 80s world. *"THE BEST COMEDY OF THE SEASON. Trenchant, dark and jagged. Newcomer Christopher Kyle is a playwright whose social satire comes with a nasty, ripping edge - Molière by way of Joe Orton." - Variety. "By far the most stimulating playwright I've encountered in many a buffaloed moon." - New York Magazine. "Smart, funny, articulate and wisely touched with rue...the script radiates a bright, bold energy." - The Village Voice.* [2M, 3W]

❏ **DURANG/DURANG by Christopher Durang.** These cutting parodies of *The Glass Menagerie* and *A Lie of the Mind,* along with the other short plays in the collection, prove once and for all that Christopher Durang is our theater's unequivocal master of outrageous comedy. *"The fine art of parody has returned to theater in a production you can sink your teeth and mind into, while also laughing like an idiot." - New York Times. "If you need a break from serious drama, the place to go is Christopher Durang's silly, funny, over-the-top sketches." - TheatreWeek.* [3M, 4W, flexible casting]

DRAMATISTS PLAY SERVICE, INC.
440 Park Avenue South, New York, New York 10016 212-683-8960 Fax 212-213-1539

TODAY'S HOTTEST NEW PLAYS

☐ **THREE VIEWINGS by Jeffrey Hatcher.** Three comic-dramatic monologues, set in a midwestern funeral parlor, interweave as they explore the ways we grieve, remember, and move on. *"Finally, what we have been waiting for: a new, true, idiosyncratic voice in the theater. And don't tell me you hate monologues; you can't hate them more than I do. But these are much more: windows into the deep of each speaker's fascinating, paradoxical, unique soul, and windows out into a gallery of surrounding people, into hilarious and horrific coincidences and conjunctions, into the whole dirty but irresistible business of living in this damnable but spellbinding place we presume to call the world."* - New York Magazine. [1M, 2W]

☐ **HAVING OUR SAY by Emily Mann.** The Delany Sisters' Bestselling Memoir is now one of Broadway's Best-Loved Plays! Having lived over one hundred years apiece, Bessie and Sadie Delany have plenty to say, and their story is not simply African-American history or women's history...it is our history as a nation. *"The most provocative and entertaining family play to reach Broadway in a long time."* - New York Times. *"Fascinating, marvelous, moving and forceful."* - Associated Press. [2W]

☐ **THE YOUNG MAN FROM ATLANTA Winner of the 1995 Pulitzer Prize. by Horton Foote.** An older couple attempts to recover from the suicide death of their only son, but the menacing truth of why he died, and what a certain Young Man from Atlanta had to do with it, keeps them from the peace they so desperately need. *"Foote ladles on character and period nuances with a density unparalleled in any living playwright."* - NY Newsday. [5M, 4W]

☐ **SIMPATICO by Sam Shepard.** Years ago, two men organized a horse racing scam. Now, years later, the plot backfires against the ringleader when his partner decides to come out of hiding. *"Mr. Shepard writing at his distinctive, savage best."* - New York Times. [3M, 3W]

☐ **MOONLIGHT by Harold Pinter.** The love-hate relationship between a dying man and his family is the subject of Harold Pinter's first full-length play since *Betrayal*. *"Pinter works the language as a master pianist works the keyboard."* - New York Post. [4M, 2W, 1G]

☐ **SYLVIA by A.R. Gurney.** This romantic comedy, the funniest to come along in years, tells the story of a twenty-two year old marriage on the rocks, and of Sylvia, the dog who turns it all around. *"A delicious and dizzy new comedy."* - New York Times. *"FETCHING! I hope it runs longer than Cats!"* - New York Daily News. [2M, 2W]

DRAMATISTS PLAY SERVICE, INC.
440 Park Avenue South, New York, New York 10016 212-683-8960 Fax 212-213-1539